PRAISE FOR *A GOOD*

'Peter Grose's tale of the astounding "rescue village" of Le Chambon
. . . is a story resonant in our days, the age of refugees, and a
grand narrative in its own right, all told with absorbing narrative
skill. A book to cherish and recommend!'

Thomas Keneally

'This is a beautifully written tribute . . . and an outstanding
contribution to Holocaust literature.'

Booklist

'Inspiring. In chronicling the daring activity that went on for
years, Grose keeps readers on the edge with a heartwarming
story of ordinary heroes who just did what was required.'

Kirkus Reviews

'. . . a page-turning account of how one French village defied
the Nazis . . .'

The Bookseller

'If you need proof that truth is stranger than fiction, go no
further than this marvellous evocation of an isolated French
village during World War II.'

Ballarat Courier

'What a terrific book. The subject matter is incredible . . . and
Peter Grose's writing style is wonderful (read: highly enjoyable) and
authoritative (read: educational). I devoured this book in two sittings
and will be snapping up everything else this author has written.'

Julie Lawson Timmer, author of *Five Days Left*

'This meticulously researched, intriguing account documents
the key figures in restrained prose that accentuates the sheer
drama of the situation, delivers a salutary and resonant tale of
a community rising to its best.'

Bendigo Advertiser

'This book's publication is perfectly timed. Yes, it's a deeply humane, diligently researched, skillfully written, and intelligently structured book. And normally these would be the strengths to mention first. But . . . when a story this human comes along, it becomes a symbol of hope.'

Lawrence J. Epstein, author of *The Basic Beliefs of Judaism*

'In the vein of *Schindler's List*, *A Good Place to Hide* combines solid historical research with the tension of a spy novel . . . an inspiring account of the extraordinary courage of ordinary people.'

Shelf Awareness

'Engrossing from beginning to end and painstakingly researched, master storyteller Peter Grose paints a vivid and moving picture of this era, leaving one with a sense of the triumph of human decency over grim odds.'

Toowoomba Chronicle

PRAISE FOR *AN AWKWARD TRUTH*

'Grose's compassionate, honest and vivid account, with its awkward truths, deserves to be widely read.'

Sun-Herald

'This intriguing book should be read by all school students and history buffs as well as by the general reader.'

Sydney Morning Herald

'A masterful piece of research, easy to read, moving and unbiased. A must read.'

Reveille

'Peter Grose tells a brilliantly researched, intriguing story of heroism, looting, bungling and ill-preparedness.'

Toowoomba Chronicle

'The truth [Grose] uncovers would be laughable if it weren't so tragic.'

Adelaide Advertiser

'Grose reveals an eye for telling detail.'

Canberra Times

'Read this engrossing book.'

Australian Defence Magazine

'Illuminating. Grose has researched meticulously. Readers will learn more than they expected.'

Townsville Bulletin

PRAISE FOR *A VERY RUDE AWAKENING*

'Peter Grose has a natural ability to tell a good yarn and the story of the Japanese subs that slid into Sydney Harbour in 1942 is about as good as any Aussie yarn can get. This is the kind of history writing that ensures the reader is engaged not only with the story but also the background drama.'

Sydney Morning Herald

'Grose knows how to write. [He] has many objectives here: to tell the story (and a fascinating one it is, too) in fine detail; to give us the political, military and social context; and to question received truths.'

The Age

'This book is an absolute cracker . . . well researched and carefully written.'

Army Magazine

'Grose has produced an absorbing and thought-provoking study of that fateful night.'

Australian Defence Review

'*A Very Rude Awakening* is a ground-breaking new look at the night in 1942 when three Japanese midget submarines crept into Sydney Harbour and caused an unforgettable night of mayhem, high farce, chaos and courage.'

Defence News

'A stylish, gripping and masterfully told reconstruction of the night of 31 May 1942.'

Asia-Pacific Defence Reporter

'Grose's spirited, well-researched book exposes much about a society at war, as well as one of the most daring military episodes in its course.'

The Bulletin

'*A Very Rude Awakening* reveals the triumphs of the little blokes doing their best while the might and pomp of high-ranking officialdom flapped about uselessly.'

RSL News

'The battle of Sydney Harbour is an enthralling story which Grose tells with verve.'

Law Society Journal

'A fascinating account of one of the more bizarre episodes from World War II.'

News Weekly

'Those with an interest in Australian history will enjoy this book immensely, primarily because it is so well written and its subject holds a strong fascination.'

Newcastle Herald

'Engrossing.'

Surfer's Paradise Weekend Bulletin

PETER GROSE began his working life as a journalist for the Sydney *Daily Mirror* before becoming the first London correspondent of *The Australian*. He switched from journalism to literary agency, setting up Curtis Brown Australia, then the first literary agency in Australia and now the biggest. After moving to the London office of Curtis Brown, where he continued as a literary agent, he joined the London publisher Martin Secker & Warburg as publishing director. In his 'retirement' he returned to his first love: writing. He is the author of three bestselling history books. He is also the proud holder of British, American and Australian private pilot's licences, and has flown all over Australia, Europe and the United States in single-engine aircraft. He lives in France.

OTHER BOOKS BY PETER GROSE

A Very Rude Awakening:
The night the Japanese midget subs came to Sydney Harbour

An Awkward Truth:
The bombing of Darwin, February 1942

A Good Place to Hide:
How one French community saved thousands
of lives in World War II

TEN
ROGUES

THE UNLIKELY STORY OF CONVICT SCHEMERS, A STOLEN BRIG AND AN ESCAPE FROM VAN DIEMEN'S LAND TO CHILE

PETER GROSE

ALLEN&UNWIN
SYDNEY·MELBOURNE·AUCKLAND·LONDON

Allen & Unwin
83 Alexander Street
Crows Nest NSW 2065
Australia
Phone: (61 2) 8425 0100
Email: info@allenandunwin.com
Web: www.allenandunwin.com

A catalogue record for this
book is available from the
National Library of Australia

ISBN 978 1 76063 261 8

Maps and illustrations by Mika Tabata
Set in 12.5/18.5 pt Adobe Garamond by Midland Typesetters, Australia
Printed and bound in Australia by Griffin Press, part of Ovato

10 9 8 7 6 5 4 3 2 1

The paper in this book is FSC® certified.
FSC® promotes environmentally responsible,
socially beneficial and economically viable
management of the world's forests.

For all those who have suffered, and those suffering today,
from the baseless belief that harsh punishment
reduces crime and reforms criminals

CONTENTS

INTRODUCTION

I never planned to tell the story of Jimmy Porter and the seizure of the brig *Frederick*.

In February 2016 my wife, Ros, and I took a week's holiday in Tasmania with my lifelong friend Richard Walsh (who also happens to be the original publisher of this book) and Richard's wife, Sue. We all met up in Hobart and drove together to the north coast of Tasmania, then down to Strahan on the west coast to take a cruise on the beautiful Gordon River.

At the time, I had a half-baked idea to write a book called *Punishment*, which would have been a history of that tortured subject and would have dealt with all those futile historical punishments, from administering hemlock to dunking witches to hanging thieves. I planned to write it with my daughter Anouchka, a London psychoanalyst who has written more books than I ever will.

If I'd stuck to this original plan, I would very likely have come up with all the usual facile liberal conclusions that punishment doesn't work, and that the best way to treat criminals is to keep them apart from the rest of society, then give them something useful to do. That was about as far as I'd got.

Then, as part of the Gordon River cruise, I visited the early nineteenth-century penal settlement of Sarah Island. It can be found in Macquarie Harbour, near the small village of Strahan. As I wandered around Sarah Island, my first reaction was that here was perfect proof of everything I believed: give those convicts a useful craft—in this case shipbuilding—while simultaneously making sure they were better fed and better housed, and discipline would improve out of all recognition. Hanging and flogging could go out of style. I began busily taking photographs of various plaques scattered around Sarah Island illustrating this transformation.

Then I came across the story of the seizure of the brig *Frederick* and the ten convicts' epic voyage to Chile and freedom. I could suddenly see the major thesis of *Punishment* gift-wrapped and packaged as an irresistible narrative. It was a story with everything: defiance of authority, an adventurous sea voyage, cheeky convicts, stuffy, sadistic and occasionally buffoonish bureaucrats, and above all a compelling tale with a happy ending. Who could ask for more? I started researching and discovered that there was a wealth of original source material easily available. For instance, the handwritten convict records from the early nineteenth century had been digitally copied and were available online, which meant they could be accessed easily from anywhere in the world.

Furthermore, my central character, Jimmy Porter, had left two first-hand accounts of his life. One was written in Hobart in 1837. The second was written on Norfolk Island in 1842. Gold dust! And the whole tale seemed to me to be the perfect anecdote to illustrate the points I had planned to make in *Punishment*.

I was well and truly under way with the new book when I was brought up short by Dr Hamish Maxwell-Stewart, Professor of History at the University of Tasmania and author of *Closing Hell's Gates*, a superb and definitive history of Sarah Island. We met over breakfast at a Balmoral cafe in Sydney's harbourside suburb of Mosman. I put forward my rather gauche theory about how some useful work in the form of shipbuilding combined with better treatment had been a more effective convict reform program than any hanging and flogging regime. This was destroyed instantly by Hamish. My theory was too facile and middle class, he thought. The reality was not that well-meaning liberals had rescued the convicts. Rather, the convicts had survived by their uncrushable spirit, which enabled them to keep going and retain their humanity and individuality despite every effort by the authorities to flatten and destroy them.

As my research dug deeper, I came to realise that Hamish was right. Yes, giving the convicts useful things to do coincided with improved discipline and a reduction of floggings and hangings. But without the convicts' remarkable refusal to be crushed and destroyed, no amount of dewy-eyed wishful thinking would have prevailed.

So, as you read the pages that follow, spare a thought for the 166,000 convicts transported from Britain to Australia between 1788 and 1868 whose stories are not told in this book. These overlooked men and women were deeply mired in injustice, bullying, and arbitrary and cruel punishment. They were patronised, demonised, dismissed with contempt, exploited and brutalised. Yet huge numbers of them managed to keep their humanity, and their spirit.

So while I can hardly deny that the main attraction of the story of the stealing of the brig *Frederick* is that it makes for a rollicking good yarn, I would also like to put in a plea for a larger truth. Human beings in general are too resilient and too spirited to be destroyed permanently by punishment, however harsh and pitiless. And somewhere in all of our DNA is a streak of optimism that allows human beings to plan for a better life rather than be put down by petty tyranny, injustice and cruelty, whatever form it takes.

While I was researching this book, I learned a lot of things I should have been taught at school, but wasn't. I had no idea of the close connection between the British convict system and the slave trade. Nor did I have any appreciation of how liberally the earliest prisoners transported to Australia were treated.

We are used to the idea of relentless inhumane treatment handed out to convicts: clapped in irons, chained, flogged and demoralised. My school lessons in Australian history gave me no inkling of the amount of freedom many convicts enjoyed, particularly in the early years of the colony. Yes, some worked in chains. But others roamed the streets freely, married, set up home and lived comparatively normal lives while still under sentence. Convicts were not usually locked in cells: most were 'assigned' to free settlers, where they were worked hard but were not always mistreated. In those early years, convicts with a track record of good behaviour could apply for a 'ticket of leave', which meant they could pick and choose their employer, and negotiate their terms of employment. For all practical purposes, they were free men and women, forced only to remain in exile for the term of their sentence. And when they had completed that sentence, they might even be eligible for a grant of land, and free convict labour to work it. Compare that with the fate of today's incarcerated drug addict or petty thief, in Australia or anywhere else in the world.

Peter Grose
August 2019

CONVICTS

Chapter 1

JIMMY

It's hard to know whether to like or dislike Jimmy Porter. He was, by his own account, a killer and a thief. He was also a deserting husband and father, and a tireless schemer and con man. His real persona bears a fair resemblance to one of those enduring heroes of popular fiction, the lovable rogue. He was a self-pitying liar, but then his survival more than once depended on his being economical with the truth. And if his survival led to a few clamorous bouts of self-promotion and fact twisting . . . well, what are lovable rogues *for*?

Jimmy Porter was born 'in the neighbourhood of London', probably in Bermondsey, a dingy inner London suburb now best known for its Friday antiques market. The year of his birth must have been around 1800, perhaps as late as 1802, but he gave the authorities several inconsistent versions of his age, so it is impossible to calculate a reliable date. He doesn't say why, but at the age of six he was placed in the care of his grandmother, 'though not without great reluctance on the part of my mother'. His time with his granny was, by his account, happy. He went to school until he was twelve, and says of himself, 'I could write a tolerable hand and was pretty forward in arithmetic.' But his rebellious streak soon had him in trouble. He recalls being punished by his schoolmaster 'for placing hair in his cane so that when he chastised any of us it would split up and cut his hand'.

Sometime towards the end of his twelfth year, Jimmy started playing truant, which marked the beginning of his misfortunes. Characteristically, he blamed this on someone else: 'I was not sufficiently checked by my grandmother,' he wrote afterwards. To make things worse, he was subject to regular thrashings by his schoolmaster—'beating *out* one devil and beating *in* two'. In the face of all this, he persuaded his grandmother to let him drop out of school. He then ran wild with the neighbouring children 'and soon got initiated into vice'. His first crime was to steal money from his granny to see a performance at the newly restored Drury Lane Theatre in Covent Garden. The stage show entranced him, and the memory of it never left him. Unfortunately it was not without cost: his grandmother's shock and anger at this piece of treachery 'hurried her to her grave'.

But not yet. Jimmy was full of remorse over his betrayal of his grandmother and vowed never to steal again. In his own words: 'Had I then been separated from my acquaintances and sent to sea under good treatment in a man o' war, it would have cured all.' That didn't happen. Instead, still running free with his young friends, he was desperate to get back to see another theatre performance. But where would he find the entrance money?

In his account, two boys put him up to the next crime. The trio passed a wealthy house, looked through the parlour window, and spotted a handsome clock on the mantelpiece. Would Jimmy come back at dusk and sneak in and grab it? Yes, he would. He managed to do as he was asked and run off with the clock, duly receiving a small share of the proceeds when it was 'fenced'. But he had been seen entering the house, and identified. He was subsequently nabbed, and taken to his grandmother, 'who swooned away'. His parents arrived to discuss the matter with the gentleman victim, who agreed not to prosecute, according to Porter, 'on the account of the respectability of my parents'. All agreed that young Jimmy's career in crime could only lead to the gallows, and the best move would be to send the lad to sea while his neck remained unstretched.

Jimmy had an uncle living in Gravesend, then an important river port on the Thames Estuary, east of London. The uncle, a ship's captain who owned a brig and a schooner,[1] was no stranger to trouble with the law; he had lost several vessels after being caught smuggling. However, he proved to be an artful dodger, and his smuggling successes outnumbered his failures to the point where he became a rich man. He was tanned, ferocious looking, and in no mood to indulge his nephew. Young Jimmy was ordered to sea in the brig *Sophia*, whose captain, he was told, would 'either make a sailor of you or an idiot'. Jimmy

---

1 A brig is a two-masted, square-rigged sailing ship. A schooner is also a two-masted sailing ship, not necessarily square-rigged, with the forward mast shorter than the rear mast.

didn't much care for any of this; he planned to run away but was not quick enough, and within a few days found himself setting out to sea in the *Sophia*, under the command of the tyrannical Captain Lindsay. His first voyage was to be long and arduous, 9271 kilometres (5761 miles) across the wild Atlantic Ocean to Rio de Janeiro.

———

Captain Lindsay proved to be as harsh as Jimmy's uncle had predicted. In Jimmy's words:

> Before I hardly knew what a ship was, I was mastheaded [made to climb to the top of the main mast, a punishment] on the most trivial occasion, where I was obliged to hold on like grim death to a topmast backstay and, worse than all, we made very bad weather and a long passage, though it was the means of making a sharp lad of me.

When they reached Rio de Janeiro, Jimmy went ashore, and didn't like what he saw: 'many Negro Slaves'. He again decided to run away. To cover his needs while on the run, he stole '50 doubloons [gold coins] and a hundred dollars from the Captain, to defray expenses'. With another of the *Sophia*'s crew, he absconded and joined the crew of a schooner anchored nearby.

> The Captain's name was Pedro Blanco, a very keen fellow. He had formerly been Captain of a Slaver. My friend, being an able seaman, received 16 dollars and small stores, and

the Captain said that if I made myself handy he would give me 12 dollars per month. I was content and remained with him for upwards of a 12 month, making several voyages with him, never caring much about going ashore until I had learned some of the language. However myself and friend left the schooner and shipped in a Barque[2] named *Anne of London* homeward bound from Rio. We received very good usage on board.

Jimmy had sailed from England in 1815 and he landed back in England in 1817. He made his way to London and was reunited with his family. He complained to his father about his treatment at the hands of Captain Lindsay, adding that he thought Lindsay had acted so brutally on the specific orders of his uncle. This led to 'harsh words' between his father and his uncle, but over time the two brothers were reconciled.

Jimmy wanted to get back to sea, and in 1818 he signed on for a three-year voyage on a whaler, *John Bull*, which would hunt for sperm whales in the waters off Peru.

I was at this time a smart lad in a ship. We had a good passage until we neared the Horn[3]—terrific seas and dreadful colds—icicles and icebergs. I never experienced any real hardship until now, the cold being almost unsupportable.

---

2 A barque is a three-masted sailing ship with square-rig sails on the forward and main masts.

3 Cape Horn, at the southern tip of South America, famous for its wild seas, furious winds and dangerous ice.

We were compelled to keep Man o' War watches for fear of the Ice. Several of the crew were injured by the cold, and it caused one man's death.

After six months' cruising, the *John Bull* put into the port of Valparaiso in Chile, to replenish supplies. Jimmy went ashore. His account of what happened next is as interesting for what he doesn't tell us as for what he reveals. We know nothing of the circumstances, but in Valparaiso he met a girl, Narcissa Martel (or Martell). He doesn't say he fell in love, nor does he tell us anything about her, though we can deduce from later events that her family was at least moderately wealthy. We know nothing of her age, her beauty, or her many other attractions. All he tells us in his journal is: 'Having a good deal of money about me, I bid farewell to the Ship, and a Spanish girl stowed me away on her father's premises until the ship sailed again.' In other words, he deserted ship and Narcissa's family hid him. He continues: 'I began to think of marriage by the continual persuasion of her friends.'

There has to be more than a suspicion that Jimmy's motives were not romantic. Being Jimmy, he must have realised that he was onto a good thing. In Chile at the time, there was a fashion among high-society girls for marrying British sailors; marrying a European was seen as marrying up. There has to be a further suspicion that Jimmy spun a good yarn about his background and prospects. He says he had plenty of money at the time, so his story would have rung true. Perhaps he told the Martels that his uncle owned a shipping line, and that Jimmy's promotion to captain of his own ship in his uncle's line could only be a matter of time.

The family wanted the couple to marry straight away, but Jimmy considered himself too young (he gives his age at the time as sixteen). So he agreed with Narcissa's father, Fernando Martel, that he would make 'a voyage or two' and then come back and marry her.

He joined the crew of an armed schooner, *Liberta*, which delivered Chilean troops to various points up and down the coast. He stayed with the *Liberta*[4] for about a year, in the course of which he necessarily learned some military skills. He says he took part in some 'skirmishes ashore', and occasionally at sea, 'giving the Spaniards a round turn from the schooner from our two Long Toms'.

After twelve months with the *Liberta* he returned to Valparaiso, and married Narcissa. There is no trace of the marriage in official records, so it is impossible to pin down a date or even a location. The best I could find was a brief reference in a genealogical paper about the Anglo-Chilean community written by L.C. Derrick-Jehu. In a long list of names of English people married to Chilean spouses there appears: 'PORTER, James:

---

4   It is a measure of the problems of accepting Jimmy's version of these and other events that there is no trace of a ship called *Liberta* in the Chilean Navy, or any other navy for that matter. However, in 1819 there was an expedition called *Expedición libertadora del Peru* ('Peruvian liberation expedition') that involved plenty of skirmishing along the Chilean and Peruvian coasts as far north as Callao, the port serving the Peruvian capital of Lima. It is possible Jimmy was part of that.

b. in London c 1800. He m. before 1830 Narcissus daughter of Fernando MARTELL of Valparaiso (P.H.).'

Whether or not the marriage was happy, Jimmy doesn't say. But it was certainly lucrative. The dowry included a farm about 21 miles (34 kilometres) from Valparaiso along the road to Santiago. Jimmy agreed with his new father-in-law that he would no longer go to sea, and he and Narcissa settled at the farm.

━━━━━━

As Chile will play a key part in this narrative, it is probably worth digressing here to gallop through a bit of nineteenth-century Chilean history. Until 1810, Chile had been an impoverished but largely peaceful part of the Spanish colonial empire. It was governed by a viceroy, who answered to the Spanish government through a more senior viceroy in Argentina. Two waves of history then came together to ruffle the waters. First, in 1806 the French under Napoleon invaded Spain and by 1808 had overthrown the monarchy of Ferdinand VII. Napoleon replaced Ferdinand with his own older brother, Joseph Bonaparte, who became King José I of Spain. This led to turmoil in the Spanish colonial empire, loosening the grip of Spain on its colonies. The resulting power vacuum inevitably encouraged warring factions to emerge from inside the colonies.

The second wave was a burgeoning movement around the world to end colonialism and secure independence for former colonies. The Americans had thrown the British out in 1776. The Haitians threw the French out in 1804. Revolutions against

Spanish rule spread across Latin America, starting with Bolivia in 1809. The Mexicans were restless. So were the Argentinians, and the Brazilians. In 1810 the Chilean authorities made the next decisive move by declaring independence, triggering irregular conflict. Some factions in Chile stayed loyal to the deposed King Ferdinand. Others thought they might as well accept Joseph Bonaparte, at least until Ferdinand could be restored to the throne. Those who rejected colonial rule and supported the new, independent government were known as Patriots, and the Patriots included Jimmy's future in-laws. The Patriots fought a scrappy civil war against the various royalist factions within Chile, as well as against the Spanish themselves.

Given that the independent Chileans were fighting the Spanish and through them the French, it hardly comes as a surprise that the British gave them some covert help. Lord Cochrane, the hero of many a naval battle in the Napoleonic Wars (Napoleon called him *le loup des mers*—'The Wolf of the Seas'), was conveniently in disgrace in England, and therefore free to pick his own fights. He led the navy of independent Chile against the Spanish during the civil war.[5] The British couldn't be seen to encourage the forces of anti-colonialism, as they had plenty of colonies of their own to cling to, but if they could give their enemies' enemies a bit of a hand, what fun!

---

5 Cochrane is thought to have been the inspiration for two twentieth-century fictional British naval heroes: C.S. Forester's Horatio Hornblower, and Patrick O'Brian's Jack Aubrey.

When the Chilean civil war was entering its sixth year, there came an event that changed everything. On 18 June 1815 Napoleon was defeated at Waterloo in Belgium, ending France's dreams of leading a European empire with satellite colonies around the world. Spain was already weak after its defeat by France. As a result, Britain became the dominant world power, and the possessor of the biggest and most imposing navy, guarding a lucrative colonial empire spanning the globe.

In Chile the Royalists were finally defeated in 1821, and Spain gave up in 1826. So the Patriots won, and Jimmy's new family found themselves on the winning side. Yet the independent Chileans had mixed feelings about the British. On the one hand, they distrusted all European powers, particularly those who maintained colonies. On the other hand, it would have been both churlish and counterproductive not to cooperate with the British when they seemed willing to offer practical help. So independent Chile's relations with Britain could be characterised in three words—warm but wary.

Jimmy Porter's life as a Chilean farmer seems to have got off to a flying start.

> I found it a most beautiful spot. Quite congenial to my feelings, and I remained happy in the new situation for upwards of two years—my wife had a boy and a girl during this time—the girl died shortly after its birth. The country was very much agitated at the time as the patriots were

contending for their independence and Lord Cochrane was very busy along the coast—scarce a man could call his life his own without being on the alert.

Jimmy does not say in either of his memoirs whether the farm was successful but nor does he complain about hard times. So we can reasonably assume that married life on the farm treated him well. However, throughout his life he displayed a spectacular gift for making terrible and self-destructive decisions, and that gift did not desert him now. Growing tired of what was almost certainly prosperous contentment on the farm, he took a decision that would wreck his life for years to come:

> I again (like Gulliver) felt an inclination to go to sea for a trip or two, and mentioned it to my wife, which gave her great uneasiness. But, having seen her Parents, with great persuasion they consented. After taking affectionate leave of my Wife and Son, I shipped on a Chilean Brig called the *Saint Juan* bound to Callao in Peru.

By the time the *Saint Juan* reached Callao, the port of the Peruvian capital of Lima, Jimmy had discovered that the ship was on a smuggling trip. He decided to jump ship. The captain went ashore, headed for Lima. Without proper leave, Jimmy went ashore too. This made him an absconder, so the military were called in to find him. What might have been a minor incident now blew up into a major disaster.

The military found me in a grog shop. The chief mate, [of the *Saint Juan*] being with them, pointed me out. I, being rather groggy with *aquadent* [a fiery alcoholic home brew much enjoyed at that time in Latin America], would not go with them. They commenced using their sabres, by order of the Mate. I then drew a sling shot[6] out of my pocket to defend myself, and a regular engagement occurred.

There being a couple of Blue Jackets[7] in the grog shop with me, they assisted me against the four. The Chief mate drew one of his country knives, he being a Frenchman. Finding I had no alternative but to fight or lose my life I let drive with my sling shot and struck the mate on the back of the head. At that moment he was about stabbing me with his knife. I bilged in his head gear [injured his head, making it bleed profusely] with the blow and he fell senseless at my feet. The two sailors that were there with me played their part and knocked down two soldiers out of the three. The other bolted. I received a slight wound in the head and one of the sailors got a severe gash in the arm. We were compelled to make our escape as quick as possible for we expected a reinforcement in pursuit of us.

---

6   A slingshot—a weapon made from a band stretched across a forked stick, and firing anything from a stone to a ball bearing—can be a fearsome device (just ask Goliath).

7   The term Blue Jacket can include almost any sailor, but in this context Jimmy's allies were probably from a British Royal Navy ship.

Jimmy hid in the streets overnight and throughout the next day. That evening he returned to the grog shop, where he could hear drunken carousing coming from some soldiers inside. Then he saw a sailor, and beckoned to him. The sailor turned out to be from the same ship as the two men who had fought alongside Jimmy the night before. Their ship was sailing the next day. Could they use an extra hand? Jimmy asked. Yes, they could. The sailor had one further piece of information. Jimmy would be well advised to ship out as quickly as possible: the chief mate whom he had hit with his slingshot was dead. His skull had been fractured. If Jimmy were caught, he would very likely be shot. So Jimmy joined the crew of the barque *Mermaid* and sailed for England.

It was not until the next day that I was stung with remorse at the very idea of leaving my wife and child behind me. I hoped I should see them once again. In the course of a fortnight or three weeks I felt a little easier in my mind and was determined that, should I reach England in safety, after having an interview with my friends, I would immediately ship for Valparaiso, consider it my native land, there to rest happy with my wife and child.

That fond hope was not to be.

━━ ━ ━━

Jimmy arrived back in England at the end of 1821, and stayed a year. He soon fell into bad company and, being short of money, opted for the last big hustle. As he tells it: 'I was persuaded to make one push which would make me rich or cost me my life.' With two accomplices, he took part in a raid on a cutter[8] anchored at Northfleet, near Gravesend on the Thames Estuary. They made off with a good haul of silk and beaver fur, and might have got away with it if one of the others had not secretly hidden some of the loot under his clothing, hoping to score a larger than fair share of the spoils. The trio made it safely as far as London, but the fraudster was caught. He then betrayed his two accomplices. All three were imprisoned, found guilty, and sentenced to death. It was something of a milestone in young Jimmy Porter's life—his first death sentence, though not his last.

Jimmy says he had planned to keep all of this from his parents and grandmother, and simply accept his fate. But the betrayer somehow got word to Jimmy's parents. 'The shock nearly cost my mother her life,' he wrote. 'But, being of strong constitution, she recovered.' Not so Jimmy's grandmother. She died with, according to Jimmy, 'my name being the last words she pronounced'. Her death came before she could be told that he was to be spared the gallows. Instead his sentence was commuted. He now faced the lesser penalty of transportation to Van Diemen's Land. For life.

---

8 A single-masted sailing ship, similar to a sloop but with its mast more to the rear.

Chapter 2

TRANSPORTATION

Without the American Revolution, the events of the story that follows might never have happened.

It all began with the concept of class, which was widely accepted in Britain in the eighteenth and nineteenth centuries as something God had ordained. There were three major classes in society: upper, middle (or merchant) and lower. There was no use arguing with it—God had already made up his mind. In the words of that dismal nineteenth-century hymn 'All Things Bright and Beautiful':

The rich man in his castle,
The poor man at his gate,
God made them high and lowly,
And ordered their estate.

There was a further class possibility. The rulers of Britain held to a simplistic belief that there was another separate and identifiable group: the criminal class. As long as this idea was accepted, the solution to the problem of criminality was obvious. If the whole criminal class could be kept at a safe distance from decent and law-abiding citizens, there would be no more crime. Job done.

The authorities set about achieving this solution in three ways. The most certain means of neutralising criminals was to kill them. Offences that might today be punished with a fine or a dose of community service could, in the seventeenth and eighteenth centuries, lead to the hangman's noose. Over 200 offences carried a mandatory death sentence. People convicted of murder were almost certain to die at the end of a rope. Non-violent criminals such as forgers, petty thieves, burglars, even people who had done nothing more than chop down a tree that wasn't theirs, could also find themselves mounting the scaffold, sometimes publicly, before being dispatched to eternity. Others were handed custodial sentences to be served in a prison or a 'hulk'. Being in custody would punish them; it would also keep them locked away from their victims, past and future.

The authorities had one more weapon: exile. This came to be known as 'transportation', and it was regarded as the second most severe punishment after hanging. From around 1610 onwards, a criminal could be spared execution and instead sentenced to a period of transportation to a distant colony, usually for a multiple of seven years. So sentences of transportation for seven or fourteen years, or for life, became part of the process of deterring and isolating criminals. In 1717 the British parliament passed the Transportation Act. Its fuller title was *An Act for the further preventing Robbery, Burglary, and other*

Felonies, and for the more effectual Transportation of Felons, and unlawful Exporters of Wool; and for declaring the Law upon some Points relating to Pirates. There was an additional sting: escaping and returning to Britain before completing the term of exile was a capital offence. So criminals sentenced to transportation might have temporarily escaped the noose, but the shadow of the hangman still loomed over them.

At first, English, Irish, Scottish and Welsh convicts sentenced to transportation were sent mostly to the American colonies, usually to Virginia and Maryland, but smaller numbers also went to Georgia, Kentucky, New Jersey, Delaware, Pennsylvania, even genteel New England. There is some dispute over the numbers, but the generally accepted figure is 52,000 criminals transported to the American colonies between 1610 and 1776. Some sources put the number as high as 120,000, but the higher figure probably includes indentured labourers[9] as well as convicts.

It is worth examining the strong connection between the practice of transportation and the widespread practice of slavery. The slave trade, sadly, continues to this day. However, it was beginning to go out of favour in Europe and its colonies by the middle of the eighteenth century. Despite this, it was not until the early nineteenth century—25 March 1807, to be precise—that the British parliament passed the Abolition of the Slave Trade Act.

---

9   Indentured labourers either offered themselves or were forced into a fixed-term contract with a particular employer. The whole practice was supposed to have been outlawed along with the abolition of slavery in the early nineteenth century. The fact that this practice ended almost 200 years ago will probably come as news to workers today with term contracts in the 'gig' economy.

And it was not until 1 August 1834 that the stronger Slavery Abolition Act came into force, making slave trading a criminal offence in Britain and its colonies. Slavery flourished alongside transportation to the American colonies. It is no coincidence that the largest group of the transported convicts—some 22,000 of them—ended up in the plantation colonies of Virginia and Maryland, where slaves were crucial to the local economy.

The British government even saw a glorious opportunity to solve the problem of criminality while making a modest profit. They took to 'selling' convicts by the boatload. Shipowners, captains and even shipbrokers paid as much as £500 for the privilege of taking a load of prisoners across the Atlantic. The captain had to enter into a bond with the British government, undertaking to ensure that the criminals he transported got to their destination to serve their sentence. On arrival, the convicts' new owner simply sold his 'passengers' as indentured labourers to the highest bidder. Women were sold as domestic servants. Lest anyone should think this was government-sponsored slavery, pure and simple, the British government wrapped up the purchase price of the convicts as reimbursement on behalf of the prisoners for gaol fees, clerks' fees, fees for the granting of a pardon (such as the commuting of a death sentence) and a whole lot of other bureaucratic flannel for what was in reality a straightforward commercial transaction.

For the colonists, transported criminals had one big advantage over regular slaves: they were cheap. A male slave might cost as much as £44. An unskilled male convict cost about £13, while women convicts were regularly sold for £7 to £14. Prices were higher for semi-skilled male convicts (around £14), and skilled males could fetch as much as £25. This was still cheaper than an unskilled slave, who would fetch about £35.[10] Furthermore, a slave was for life, whereas a transported convict might expect to walk free in as little as seven years. This largely accounted for the convicts' lower prices. The convicts worked alongside the slaves, carrying out the same tasks.

The convicts were often transported in former slave ships. The voyage lasted about six weeks and was an unmitigated horror story. Some captains set out to maximise their profits by failing to feed or water their charges. This turned out to be a short-term view: the convicts fetched a better price if they arrived in good condition. A sentence of transportation meant that the government confiscated not only the prisoner's freedom but also his or her work capacity, which could be sold for profit. It was perfect: no need to go to the expense of staffing a hulk or prison, and no need to pay for the prisoner's upkeep. Best of all, there would be a gigantic wall of impassable ocean between the prisoner and home, so he or she posed no threat to the decent and God-fearing folk who remained behind.

---

10 These numbers are far from certain. Currency equivalence is difficult to calculate at the best of times, and historical rates going back this far are nigh on impossible. The early British colonies used foreign currencies such as Spanish dollars as well as British pounds, and even bartered goods like rum when normal currency wasn't available. However, we know from probate records (slaves were property, after all) that a healthy slave in mid-eighteenth-century America cost an average of US$700, which would be about US$25,000 at today's prices. Slaves weren't cheap.

The British government's win–win situation came to a jarring halt in 1776, when the American colonies rebelled and threw the British out. The newly independent Americans had never liked the idea of importing droves of British criminals into their neighbourhoods, and they made it very clear that they had no intention of accepting any more. So what was England to do? Whatever it was, it had to be done soon, or the prisons would overflow. For a while criminals were sent to 'hulks', decommissioned merchant and naval vessels anchored in harbours or rivers and no longer fit for use as freighters or fighting ships. But the existing hulks were rapidly filling, and overcrowding was becoming rife. There had to be another solution.

Between 1768 and 1771 Captain James Cook had made his epic voyage to the southern oceans, in the course of which he 'discovered' Australia and claimed it for the British Crown. Of course, the Aboriginal people had 'discovered' and settled in Australia as much as 80,000 years earlier, and an assortment of Dutch, Portuguese and even other English navigators had 'discovered' the same land mass more than a hundred years before Cook. However, they had done nothing about it, so Australia, or New Holland, or whatever anybody cared to call it, looked like a wide-open space crying out to be filled. The British government decided to populate it with criminals. Which is how it was that on 13 May 1787, eleven years after the American colonies had successfully closed their gates to transported British criminals, a fleet of eleven ships under the command of Captain Arthur Phillip and carrying around 775 convicts set off from Portsmouth for Botany Bay.

The intention was to establish a self-sufficient colony, and to do this before the French could do the same. The British planned to build their settlement entirely with convict labour: there were no free men aboard the fleet, only convicts and their soldier and marine gaolers. Some 200 convict women sailed with the fleet.

The race to keep out the French turned out to be a close-run thing. Four days after the bulk of the First Fleet arrived in January 1788, two French ships under the command of Jean-François de Galaup, Comte de La Pérouse, sailed into Botany Bay, without convicts but with the intention of claiming the territory for France. The British received them with great courtesy and a simple message: too late, mate, we got here first. The French had to be content with having the Sydney suburb of La Perouse named in their honour. On the opposite side of Botany Bay is the suburb of Sans Souci, a French rendering of the common Australian reassurance 'no worries!'[11]

———

There was plenty to worry about in the fledgling colony. It was quickly apparent that Botany Bay was shallow and offered

---

11 La Pérouse and his two ships remained in Botany Bay for six weeks, unmolested by the British. They sailed on 10 March 1788, and were never heard from again. The wrecks of both ships were finally identified in 2005 on a reef off Vanikoro, one of the Solomon Islands. They probably fell victim to a tropical storm. There is a final irony to this story. A sixteen-year-old Corsican named Napoleon Bonaparte had volunteered for the La Pérouse mission. He was rejected. One can only wonder how different European history might have been if he had sailed with the expedition and perished with the rest of La Pérouse's crew.

poor anchorage. Worse still, the soil around Botany Bay was low quality and unsuitable for agriculture, and there was a shortage of fresh water. Finally, the local Gadigal clan were understandably suspicious about the sudden arrival of strangers.

So, time to move on. Phillip formed a scouting party and set off northwards in three open boats to look for a more suitable site. The scouts reported a fine harbour only 12 kilometres to the north, with a source of fresh water. The fleet upped anchor and set off for Port Jackson, or Sydney Harbour as it is better known.

Now that the sea voyage was over, Arthur Phillip ceased to be a mere captain of a Royal Navy vessel and became Governor Phillip of the newly founded colony of New South Wales. He wisely realised that his domain would be ungovernable unless it was governed reasonably fairly. So he agreed that marines and male convicts should have the same rations: each week they received 7 pounds (3.2 kilograms) of beef or 4 pounds (1.8 kilograms) of pork, 3 pints (1.7 litres) of dried peas, 6 ounces (170 grams) of butter, either 7 pounds of bread or 7 pounds of flour, and either an additional pound (450 grams) of flour or a half a pound (225 grams) of rice. Given that the convicts were expected to carry out hard physical work, it was hardly an adequate diet. Women received two-thirds of the men's rations, and children usually one-third.

With great difficulty, the colony survived. Ships arrived infrequently with meagre fresh supplies. Nevertheless animals bred; crops sprang up; so did buildings, first for the officers, then for the soldiers and marines, and finally for the convicts.

Streets were laid down, and bridges built. Arthur Phillip proved to be an enlightened and visionary man.

Still, this was a prison, pure and simple. The convicts were hemmed in by an inhospitable landscape where they faced starvation and might expect to encounter hostile locals. If they chose instead to escape by sea, the fourth wall of their prison was a wide and lethal ocean. They were poorly fed, and driven to work hard. Discipline was tough. A man could be flogged until all the flesh had been cut from his back for 'insolence'. Convicts who fell foul of authority worked in labour gangs, weighed down by brutal leg-irons.

The first free settlers arrived in Sydney on 16 January 1793, aboard the transport ship *Bellona*. There were twelve in all: a Dorset farmer, Thomas Rose, with his wife, niece and four children, a married couple accompanied by their adult nephew, and two other single men (one of whom promptly married the niece). Several of them had been crew on the First Fleet. Each had been promised a free passage to the colony, a grant of land when they got there, free farming tools, free convict labour, and two years' provisions. The government kept its word. Thomas Rose's family received a grant of 120 acres (49 hectares), the married men received 80 acres each, and the single men 60 acres each.

As more settlers arrived, all of them claiming a grant of land and free convict labour, a system sprang up that had much to recommend it. Before the free settlers arrived, the convicts worked for the government. They cleared land, built roads and houses, and did their best under supervision as farmers. In general, if they had a skill they were invited to use it. So farmers farmed, stonemasons chipped stones, blacksmiths forged, bakers baked, tanners tanned, brickmakers made bricks and in the fullness of time a solitary convict architect began drawing plans.

The convicts were largely free to move about the colony, as long as they did their work and stayed out of trouble. This made possible a remarkably liberal prison policy. Most of the convicts had been sentenced to be transported for a fixed term, usually seven or fourteen years. At first they were simply the property of the government, there to be ordered about, flogged when thought necessary, and worked hard. The arrival of free settlers gave rise to a system known as 'assignment'. A convict would be assigned to a free settler who, in return for supplying the prisoner with food and a roof over his head, had the free use of his labour. If the convict displeased the settler by not working hard enough, or giving cheek, or trying to run away, the settler would report him to the authorities, who would then discipline him—with the lash, or with a spell in the work gangs. Meanwhile, the settler received a replacement convict. The settler was responsible for making sure the convict behaved himself, worked hard, and didn't abscond.

Beyond this, a well-behaved convict could apply for a 'ticket of leave'. This was a much freer arrangement than 'assignment'. Rather than being tied to one settler, which in practice amounted to being chosen by the settler with no say in the matter, a ticket-of-leave prisoner could choose his settler. He would still have to work, and not abscond, but it was possible for the convict to negotiate his working conditions. With freedom of choice, a convict might now demand a little pay, or better rations, or better accommodation, or even a tolerant attitude to petty misdemeanours. Tickets of leave created a market for the convict's labour. Convicts could marry, and set up home. Better still, once his sentence had been served, the newly freed convict could apply for a grant of land. It was not automatically given, but it was an enticing possibility.

———

The threat posed by the French remained high in the minds of Governor Phillip and the new colonists in the early years of the colony. In particular, there was a fear that they would occupy Norfolk Island, a lonely rock in the mid-Pacific about 1600 kilometres from Sydney. Why would anyone want Norfolk Island? In the 21st century, it is hard for us to think of wood as a strategic resource. But from the sixteenth century onwards, oak in particular was the uranium of its day. Ships were built with wood, and ships were essential for winning wars, trading and colonising. Strong wood meant a strong nation. In 1588, when a Spanish armada set out to invade England, one of King Philip II's orders to his ambassador was to 'leave not a single tree standing in the Forest of Dean'. The Forest of Dean, on the border between England and Wales, was a primary source of oak, which was a famously superb shipbuilding material and one of the essential elements in England's rise as a world power. James Cook, when he passed by Norfolk Island, had noted dense forests of tall, straight Norfolk Island pines. Ideal for ship masts and crosstrees, he thought.

So Governor Phillip was under orders to secure Norfolk Island as quickly as possible, before the French got it. As early as March 1788, with the Sydney settlement barely two months old, Phillip sent Lieutenant Philip Gidley King to Norfolk Island in a single ship, the *Supply*, with a party of fifteen convicts. As a military foraging exercise, this turned out to be a complete waste of time. Norfolk Island pine proved to be brittle and totally unsuitable as ship's timber. The island was more promising as a place to grow a flax-like plant imported from New Zealand, but this proved difficult to weave. Finally, Norfolk Island became slightly more successful as a farm, supplying desperately needed fresh vegetables for Sydney. As a strategic asset it was a failure. Given the distances involved, as a farm it was not much better. However, it established an important precedent: the Sydney settlement could act as a base on the far side of the world for enlarging the British colonial empire. The convicts were an ideal workforce: trapped and unwilling, but with little choice other than to obey. They could do the hewing and hacking, build the roads and bridges, raise the crops, erect the buildings, all on the cheap. But before Britain's interests could spread, the continent needed to be secured.

Chapter 3

EXPANSION

George Bass, a ship's surgeon, and Matthew Flinders, a Royal Navy officer and trained navigator, met on the HMS *Reliance* on their way to Australia. They arrived in Sydney in 1795 but it was not until 1798, ten years after the settlement of Sydney, that they sailed from Sydney in the sloop HMS *Norfolk*, and circumnavigated Tasmania, then known as Van Diemen's Land. Until their voyage, nobody knew for sure whether Tasmania was an island or part of the mainland. Now everybody knew that it was separated from the mainland by Bass Strait, named in honour of its discoverer. This made Van Diemen's Land an ideal site for a convict settlement. If Sydney was escape-proof, Van Diemen's Land was even more so. However, it also created a legal problem. Both Cook and Phillip had claimed the *mainland* for the British crown. If Van Diemen's Land was a separate and substantial island, it would have to be claimed separately.

Nevertheless, there was a five-year delay before the next move. In October 1803 a party of 300 convicts under the command of Colonel David Collins arrived directly from England at

Port Phillip Bay, the site of the present city of Melbourne, and began setting up a new colony. Around the same time, 23-year-old Lieutenant John Bowen established a settlement on the Derwent River, on the east coast of Van Diemen's Land. His original settlers included 21 male and three female convicts, plus a party of marines to guard them, and a handful of free settlers. Young Lieutenant Bowen was not in charge for long. Things had not worked out well at Port Phillip Bay. It turned out to be another Botany Bay, with poor anchorage, poor water supplies and poor timber. Collins decided it had to be abandoned. He and his party of soldiers and convicts packed up and headed south to join Bowen on the banks of the Derwent River.

Collins arrived at the site of the fledgling Van Diemen's Land colony on 16 February 1804. As a colonel, he outranked Bowen, and he did not like what he found. Collins had been part of the First Fleet that arrived in Sydney in 1788, and he had some experience with setting up colonies. He disapproved of Bowen's choice of site for the settlement, and made three trips along the Derwent River before deciding on Sullivans Cove, 5 miles (8 kilometres) downriver from the original settlement, and on the opposite river bank. On 21 February the settlement moved to the new site, and the city of Hobart was born.

At first the new settlement in Van Diemen's Land simply took a spill of convicts from Sydney, plus the Port Phillip Bay refugees. However, as the new settlement became established, the British sent convicts there directly. After all, it was a slightly shorter voyage from England to Van Diemen's Land than to Sydney, and by securing another island, the British empire could be extended, and the French kept at bay. The first convicts sent directly from England arrived in Hobart in 1812. More free settlers followed in 1816. Van Diemen's Land continued to be governed from Sydney, with a Sydney-appointed but largely independent lieutenant-governor in place in Hobart, until 1825, when it separated from Sydney and became a colony in its own right, with its own governor.

George Arthur, the despotic but tidy-minded governor of Van Diemen's Land from 1824 to 1836, categorised convicts into seven groups. At the top of the heap were the ticket-of-leavers, who represented about 10 per cent of the convict population. Next in the pecking order were the assigned convicts, who comprised about half of the convict population. So some 60 per cent of convicts enjoyed quite a bit of freedom, and the government was spared the expense of feeding, clothing, housing and supervising them.

Just below the two groups of comparatively 'free' convicts came two more of Arthur's groups. The first consisted of those employed by the government on public works such as the construction of buildings and bridges. Of slightly inferior status was a second government group, which worked in road-building gangs. These two groups together accounted for a further 20 per cent of convicts. Being sent to work in one or other of the labour gangs was often a punishment. Convicts on the gangs were generally locked up at night in desperately uncomfortable cells or barracks, and were treated badly.

The remaining 20 per cent were the incorrigibles. In descending order, they were: convicts sentenced to labour in chains (about 5 per cent); those convicted of a fresh crime while still serving their sentence of transportation, who were generally then sentenced to hard labour in a separate and harsher penal settlement; and those who had been sentenced to hard labour in a separate penal settlement, and who had additionally been sentenced to work there in chains.

A newly arrived male convict in Sydney or Hobart could expect to start his sentence by working for the government on either a public building program or a road gang. That was pretty arduous. A convict could then improve his lot by working up through the system. There were also rewards: convicts who had performed some brave act or some outstanding service could be rewarded with a reduced sentence or even a full pardon. The promised land was ticket of leave. Beyond even that nirvana, convicts who had served their term of transportation were officially free, and were said to be 'emancipated'.

Many of the convicts passed through this system relatively unscathed: they were never flogged, nor hanged, nor made to work in chains. That was the carrot. Inevitably, there was also a stick. A convict who chose to defy the system or, worse, commit a new crime—such as absconding—would descend into a man-made hell of locked and cramped living quarters, semi-starvation and backbreaking labour, usually after 'retransportation' to a remote and harsher penal settlement. A flogging was usually thrown in for good measure.

While travelling down the west coast of Van Diemen's Land on their epic circumnavigation voyage, Bass and Flinders entirely missed the narrow entrance to a very promising harbour. It was an understandable miss: they were battling typically terrible west coast weather at the time, and were naturally concentrating on surviving the waves rather than admiring the view. However, in December 1815, seventeen years later, James Kelly and a crew of oarsmen in a whaleboat from Hobart became the first Europeans to enter and explore the harbour while searching for good timber. They named it Macquarie Harbour after the then governor of New South Wales, Lachlan Macquarie. Kelly gathered a few samples of timber from around Macquarie Harbour, brought them back to Hobart, and handed them to the local merchant T.W. Birch, who had paid for the expedition. Birch was delighted.

What Birch knew was that, eleven years earlier, in 1804, the crew of the whaler *Alexander* had entered the D'Entrecasteaux Channel on the southeast coast of Van Diemen's Land, and noticed some pine logs trapped in mud. The logs had clearly been in the water for years, yet they had not rotted and were not riddled by termites. They had resisted even the ferocious screw worm, or marine borer, the scourge of wooden ships everywhere. That made them ideal ship timbers. The Huon River flows into the D'Entrecasteaux Channel, so the trees came to be known as Huon pines. When it was realised that this was probably the finest shipbuilding timber in the world, as tough as oak but easier to manage, the wood was much in demand.

The Huon pine is unique to Tasmania, and what Kelly had discovered at Macquarie Harbour was the biggest and most prolific collection of Huon pines on the entire island. It was a find comparable to striking gold, or oil. The forest lined the banks of the Gordon River, which meant the logs could be cut and floated down the river for collection in Macquarie Harbour. Here was a resource ripe for exploitation.

The Huon pine was not the only attraction of Macquarie Harbour. Being on the west coast of Van Diemen's Land, it was 300 kilometres by land from Hobart Town, and separated by high mountains wrapped in thick forest. An overland journey would be impossible. The only way was by sea. Tasmanian weather is notoriously fierce, particularly on the west coast, so a fair-sized ship would be needed to handle the wind and waves. Yet there was a treacherous sandbar across the entrance to Macquarie Harbour, which meant that any ship attempting to enter or leave could not be too big or heavy, and would need skilled sailors to manage it. Put all of this together and the conclusion was obvious: any penal settlement based there would be completely escape-proof. What better place to send absconders, recidivists and the worst of the worst?

Governor Arthur set out the policy in plain and typically despotic language. Convicts sent to Macquarie Harbour could expect 'unceasing labour, total deprivation of Spirits, Tobacco and Comforts of any kind . . . the sameness of occupation, the dreariness of situation must, if anything will, reform the most vicious characters'.

In other words, there were to be no carrots, only sticks.

As we have seen, under the prevailing theories on crime and punishment in Britain and its colonies in the early nineteenth century, deterrence was the key. Hangings and floggings could take place in public, a terrifying demonstration of the consequences of flouting the law. Beyond that, the authorities set out to 'break the spirit' of those who refused to conform. In the enclosed world of a penal settlement, the superintendent wielded absolute power. His principal weapons were flogging and solitary confinement: flogging humiliated and weakened the offender; solitary confinement drove the victim to the edge of madness. In a cruel twist, the authorities decreed that convicts were to be flogged by fellow prisoners. That would stop them from getting too close to each other.

Insolence could lead to a flogging. So could 'rebelliousness' or 'neglect of work'. Losing an item of government-issue clothing could lead to a spell on the flogging triangle. Breaking a saw, axe, spade or oar, even accidentally, automatically brought 50 lashes.

At Macquarie Harbour, floggings were an almost daily occurrence. A convict named Davies wrote about a typical flogging:

> The moment it was over unless it were at Meal Hours or Nights he was immediately sent back to work, his back like Bullock's Liver and most likely his shoes full of Blood, and not permitted to go to the Hospital until next morning when his back would be washed by the Doctor's Mate and a little Hog's Lard spread on with a piece of Tow, and so

off to work . . . and it often happened that the same man
would be flogged the following day for Neglect of Work.

This brutality was part of a conscious policy. The authorities
wanted Macquarie Harbour's reputation to strike fear into the
hearts of all. They wanted to send a message loud and clear:
don't do anything that will get you sent to Macquarie Harbour.
In particular, don't try to abscond, and don't reoffend.

Yet it was not as though those sent to the settlement were
the most dangerous criminals. Only 3 per cent of the Macquarie
Harbour prisoners had committed crimes of violence. Just under
half the prisoners were sent there for theft of some kind, often
trivial. John Mawer was sentenced to seven years at Macquarie
Harbour for stealing a loaf of bread; Samuel Jones was sentenced
to two years for stealing a few sheets of paper, value two pence.
There was a suspicion among the convicts that prisoners were
sent there because they had some badly needed skill; experienced
sailors were particularly at risk.

For a Macquarie Harbour convict there would be no soft
options such as assignment or a ticket of leave. The underfed,
poorly clothed and housed convicts would work from dawn to
dark, often in chains. There would be no concessions: everything
would be done by convict hands. No animals would be used
to drag heavy logs to the river bank, or pull a plough: fields
would be tilled by hand, with hoes, picks and shovels wielded
by convicts.

The authorities' particular concern was that no one should
escape. They chose to build the main settlement on a small island

well into Macquarie Harbour called Sarah Island—named after the wife of T.W. Birch, who had funded the original expedition that found the harbour. It was generally known as Settlement Island, or sometimes Headquarters Island. Half a mile (about a kilometre) east of Sarah Island was a second, smaller island called Grummet Island, usually referred to as Small Island, which also formed part of the convict settlement. Davies, the convict who had described the flogging, wrote:

> It was a perpendicular Rock Fifty Foot above the levil [*sic*] of the sea about 40 yards long and 8 wide—a rude stairs in the cliffs is the only road to a truly Wretched Barracks Built with Boards and Shingles (the timber quite green) into which 79 men were often confined in so crowded a state as to be scarcely able to lie down on their sides—to lay on their backs was out of the question.

The authorities deliberately set out to make Macquarie Harbour a living hell. No one—soldier or convict—would ever want to go there. And no one who went there would want to return. A convict with some classical education named it 'Pluto's Land', after the Roman god of the dead. The narrow and treacherous entrance to the harbour was known as Hell's Gates. The name may have described a navigational hazard, but it also aptly described the nightmare ahead for those who made the fateful crossing.

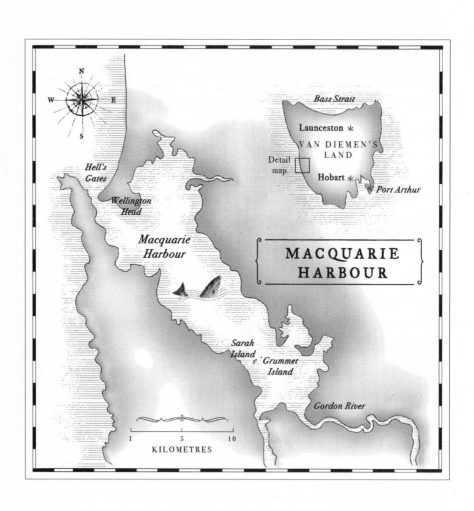

Bass Strait

Launceston ✳

VAN DIEMEN'S
LAND

Detail
map

Hobart ✳

Port Arthur

Hell's
Gates

Wellington
Head

Macquarie
Harbour

MACQUARIE
HARBOUR

Sarah
Island

Grummet
Island

Gordon River

1   5   10

KILOMETRES

After receiving his sentence for theft in London in 1823, Jimmy Porter was first sent to the hulks where, according to his account, 'Work and Usage made me often contemplate Suicide'. He was soon transferred to the convict ship *Asia* and, with 249 other convicts, set off on 28 August 1823 for Van Diemen's Land.

The convicts were locked and barricaded in semi-darkness below decks, often in chains, and poorly fed and exercised. Below decks could be stifling and facilities were basic. Jimmy was luckier than most, however: his experience as a sailor proved to be his salvation. 'The Captain released me out of irons sooner than most of the other prisoners, and I helped to work ship, being allowed the ration and grog of a seaman.'

The convict ships are a study in themselves. The British Royal Navy operated the First Fleet of convicts transported to New South Wales, so it was a government-managed affair and functioned under Royal Navy rules and discipline. But as the numbers of convicts sentenced to transportation increased, so did the numbers of ships needed, and the task of moving the prisoners halfway around the world was simply beyond the Royal Navy's stretched resources. This was particularly true in the period between 1803 and 1815, when the Royal Navy was preoccupied by the war with Napoleon. So the task of transporting the convicts was privatised from the Second Fleet of 1790 onwards.

The system was reasonably straightforward. After a court had sentenced a group of prisoners to transportation, the clerk of the court had to find 'a fit person or persons' to accept delivery of the convicts and undertake to transport them to the Australian colonies. In practice, this meant finding a shipbroker who could organise the chartering of a suitable transport vessel.

At first the courts were none too picky about who was and wasn't considered a 'fit person'. From as far back as the Second Fleet, the bulk of the early charters were awarded through a company of shipbrokers called Camden, Calvert & King, who had been the largest slave traders in London. They already had access to ships with secure below-decks accommodation, including chains and manacles. They were ideal. As we have seen, the British government passed its first anti-slavery law in March 1807, but the more forward-looking businessmen of Camden, Calvert & King had already realised that they needed to reposition themselves in the market. Transporting convicts looked like a good fit, and they switched.

They did not keep their near monopoly for long. According to ship's records, Jimmy Porter was sentenced on 26 April 1823. The search for a 'fit person' to transport him seems to have taken a little time, but by 26 July Thomas Shelton, the clerk of the Court of Sessions in the City of London, had found Joseph Lachlan, shipbroker, of Great Alie Street, Goodmans Fields,[12] in the county of Middlesex, who was willing to take on the work. The two men agreed a contract, which is reproduced as Appendix I of this book. The effect of the document was to hand over ownership of the convicts and their services forthwith to Lachlan, who gave an undertaking that he would

---

12 Great Alie Street in London seems to have been reduced to mere Alie Street today, and Goodmans Fields is now better known as Whitechapel.

transport them to Australia and hand them and all title to them to Governor Sir Thomas Brisbane in New South Wales. The document went on to say that the convicts had been loaded on board 'a certain ship or vessel called the "Asia" of which James Landsay[13] is Master and Commander which said ship is now lying at Woolwich bound to New South Wales'. The convicts were to be transported 'to the Coast of New South Wales or some one or other of the Islands adjacent'.

The shipbroker—not the captain, note—agreed to 'forthwith take and receive the said Convicts and transport them or cause them to be transported effectually as soon as conveniently might be' to New South Wales. Annexed to the contract was an eight-page list of the convicts' names, together with where and when they were convicted, and their sentence. It was a cargo manifest, pure and simple. The document includes one remarkable clause. The shipbroker was required to 'procure such evidence as the nature of the case would admit of the landing there of the said convicts (death or casualties by sea excepted) and produce the same to whom it might concern when lawfully called upon'. In other words, the captain would have to bring back proof that he had actually transported the convicts, and that they had arrived at the correct destination. However, he need not account for the dead.

Payment for transporting the convicts was calculated by the number loaded, not the number who arrived still breathing.

---

13 In other documents the master and commander of the *Asia* is referred to as James Lindsay, and elsewhere as J. Lindzee. At a guess, his correct name was James Lindsay.

The agreed fee was usually set at around £18 a head. Provisions were also calculated on the basis of convicts loaded. So the captain had a direct interest in losing a few convicts along the way. He would be paid the same whatever happened to his cargo. Further, any unused rations could then be sold on arrival at extortionate prices to the settlers in the colony.

The attrition rate was often horrific. The worst voyage was the Second Fleet, which left Portsmouth on 19 January 1790: of the 1006 reasonably healthy convicts who sailed, 267 died at sea. When the ships of the Second Fleet landed in Sydney, the captains of two of them set up a market ashore and sold a generous quantity of spare food and clothing to the residents, for what must have been a handy personal profit.

Jimmy Porter says the voyage of the *Asia* was uneventful until they reached the Cape of Good Hope on the southern tip of South Africa, traditionally the last stop before Australia. The man at *Asia*'s wheel appears to have nodded off and let the wind put the ship into reverse. Fortunately, 'the quick command of the Captain and the activity of the crew soon put all to right'. After replenishing supplies at Cape Town, the ship resumed its voyage. Four months and two days after leaving Portsmouth, the *Asia* and its convict cargo arrived at Hobart Town. They anchored off the Battery, now better known as Battery Point, the southern arm of Hobart harbour.

As was normal, the convicts remained on the ship for a few days before being taken ashore. After landing, the convicts' names and details (including a physical description) were entered into a muster roll, which also served as proof that the ship's captain and broker had delivered the convicts, and to the right place. It is possible to view Jimmy Porter's original entry on the website of the Archive Office of Tasmania. Anyone so minded will discover some neat handwriting recording that James Porter, otherwise convict P324 (the three hundred and twenty-fourth convict to arrive in Hobart whose name began with P) was nineteen years old, 5 feet 2 inches (157 centimetres) tall, with brown eyes, a beer machine maker by trade, who had been tried in Kingston, near London, in March 1823 and sentenced to transportation for life. He was reported to be a native of the London suburb of Bermondsey. For good measure, the description concluded with his distinguishing marks: he was blind in the left eye, had two scars on his forehead, a dimple on his chin, a mole on the front of his neck, and a scar on the left side of his neck. An indecipherable final line of the description might read 'pugalists [sic] on left arm', suggesting some kind of tattoo depicting boxers. The muster entry also records that James Porter was the 109th convict unloaded from the Asia in Hobart. He had been part of a Surrey Special Gaol Delivery. His date of conviction is given as 30 December 1822.

The whole fiasco is an insight into the character of Jimmy Porter, as well as a fine example of the incompetence of the authorities. He was not blind in one eye, there is no such trade as 'beer machine maker', and he was certainly older than nineteen. According to the Asia's cargo manifest, he was not convicted on

30 December 1822, nor tried in Kingston in March 1823, but convicted and sentenced in London on 26 April 1823.

There was some reasoning behind all this nonsense. The partial blindness Jimmy claimed might have led to lighter work. A non-existent skilled trade might keep him away from the labour gangs. An earlier date for his conviction could set the clock running earlier for his eventual release. And his self-proclaimed youth might lead the authorities to go a bit easier on him. As he had before and would since, Jimmy lied like a teenager who has just crashed the family car for the fifth time. Lying had become an unbreakable habit, as well as an effective survival tactic.

It may have worked. The next brief stage in Porter's new life as a transported convict was a matter of marking time. Rather than being sent at once to a work gang, he spent a few days in Hobart Gaol awaiting 'assignment'.

Part 2

VAN DIEMEN'S LAND

Chapter 4
HOBART

What sort of town did convict P324 find himself transported to? Hobart was now twenty years old. From a population of 433—mostly convicts—in 1803 it had now hit the dizzy heights of 5000. The free settler population of Van Diemen's Land had received a boost in 1808 when more than 500 people arrived from Norfolk Island, over 90 per cent of them free men and women, including many former convicts who had served their term of transportation in New South Wales and on Norfolk Island. Now they were ready for a grant of land and some free convict labour to help build a new life. By 1810 the population had risen to about 2500, still mostly soldiers and convicts but with an increasing number of free settlers, until it had reached 5000 by 1823.

Contemporary paintings and etchings show that Hobart in the 1820s was not exactly a bustling metropolis. There were some fairly substantial stone buildings, including St David's Church, Government House, and the hospital, barracks and gaol. Otherwise the town area was little more than a series of open fields crisscrossed by dirt roads. These linked the commissariat store, the stockyard, the lumberyard, and the Mulgrave Battery, as well as providing access to the neighbouring farms. An 1821 copperplate print sketch of the town shows three square-rigged sailing ships—two two-masters and one three-master—anchored off Battery Point. Cattle graze in the foreground of one of the paintings, scarcely a mile from the town centre. European-style hedges mark the boundaries of fields, and some stone cottages are dotted about, though contemporary records show that by 1810 Hobart boasted some 150 dwelling houses. The land has mostly been cleared of trees, but the scene looks for all the world like one of those middle-distance landscape paintings of a sleepy English village with a church, a few scattered houses, and a village green, all surrounded by farmland.

The free settlers were granted land, but the system of grants was chaotic and legally dubious. At the outset, all land in Van Diemen's Land was deemed to be the property of the Crown, never mind the fact that this ignored any rights of the original Aboriginal land-owners. The government granted leases for larger or smaller plots of Crown land, either for agricultural use or for dwelling. In theory, this granting of leases was done in Sydney, but in practice it was done in Hobart by the lieutenant-governor of the time, usually the most senior soldier there. Sometimes the grant was conferred in writing, but at other times it was just issued verbally. The conveyancing process was a shambles. Before the arrival of Lieutenant-Governor William Sorell in 1817, no complete records were kept. Until well into the 1820s, there were no solicitors in Hobart to ensure that titles and leases were legally sound. A few convicts had some legal training and did their best, but they were well meaning rather than competent. There were endless disputes, claims and counterclaims. The following notice is typical. It appeared in the 22 June 1827 issue of the *Hobart Town Gazette*:

> Caution: The public are cautioned against purchasing a grant of land from a person named George Hodgetts, situate at the Long Meadow near Launceston between the farms of Prosser and Townsend, the same being long since purchased and paid for by me.
>
> Ed French.

Nevertheless, Hobart Town in the 1820s did its job well. And what was its job? It was a prison, and a good one. There may have been no prison walls to scale, but beyond the town was dense bush backed by high mountains. An absconding convict might expect to starve to death or be speared by the local Aboriginal people, who perfectly reasonably saw the new arrivals as invaders, and violent ones at that. The few convicts who escaped and survived usually formed themselves into roving armed gangs of thieves, known as bushrangers. They were mercilessly hunted by the army and the constabulary, and once caught, convicted and hanged. The only serious chance of long-term escape was by sea, either by stowing away on a departing ship, or by stealing a vessel.

One other possible haven needs mention. A convict who stole a boat might do well for himself by linking up with whalers or sealers. Whaling was a huge industry in the early nineteenth century. Whales were already hunted in the Atlantic, and in the Pacific along the west coast of South America. The opening up of Australia to European settlement, and all the stories of whales in abundance, attracted whalers from all over the world, notably from America. The whales migrated up from the Antarctic in winter, looking for warmer water around Australia. When the first settlers arrived in Hobart, there were some 60 whales in the Derwent River, and it was thought to be unsafe to cross the river in a small boat for fear of encountering hostile whales.

Whaling was hard and dangerous work, and whalers were a tough and lawless bunch. They set up land-based 'whaling stations' along the east coast of Van Diemen's Land at Recherche Bay, Bruny Island, Forestier Peninsula, Maria Island, Spring Bay, Freycinet Peninsula, Bicheno and Hobart itself, and on the west coast at Port Davey. Otherwise the whaling ships roamed the seas and visited land only to replenish supplies and sell their products.

The whalers had a strong interest in keeping out of sight of the authorities. Until 1813, the ubiquitous British East India Company had a monopoly on trade in the Far East, and this monopoly was deemed to include Australia, which meant that direct trade between the colony and Britain by anyone other than the East India Company was illegal. Even when the restrictions were lifted, the British government imposed high tariffs on colonial imports of whaling products, leaving British Atlantic traders at a massive advantage. Compounding this, in 1813 the colonial government in New South Wales and Van

Diemen's Land introduced hefty duties and port charges at source. So the whalers were naturally keen to operate out of sight and outside the law. If an absconding convict was able to make contact with whalers, particularly a convict who was also an experienced seaman, there was a good chance he would be taken in and no questions asked.

———

Jimmy Porter had a very clear idea of the kind of assignment he sought. He wanted to avoid a 'dungaree settler'—a small-cropping dirt farmer who would work him from sunrise to sunset on short rations. He would prefer to stay in the town, but that was an almost universal ambition among prisoners, so he would be competing in a crowded field. Another prisoner suggested that he claim he was a skilled tradesman, and proposed the trade of whitesmith:[1] If this was believed it would guarantee him good working conditions. Jimmy then devised what followers of the *Blackadder* TV series will instantly recognise as a 'cunning plan': he asked his fellow prisoner to tell the prison superintendent that Jimmy was a good tradesman but that he would be sure to deny his trade because he no longer wished to work in it. This, he thought, would virtually guarantee that the superintendent would assign him to work in that trade.

The plan met with mixed success. A settler seeking an assigned convict came to Jimmy and asked him: 'Are you a smith?' Jimmy

---

1 A whitesmith works with white metals such as tin or galvanised iron, or does finishing work on metals.

said he wasn't. The master replied: 'Never mind, I'll chance you. I can tell by your looks you are a tradesman.' So Jimmy was assigned. The only flaw in this otherwise well-executed plan was that the new master turned out to be a blacksmith, not a whitesmith.

> I went home with him. His name was Mr Pulling. I done no work that day but the next morning I was conducted into the blacksmith's shop where his other man was getting a welding heat ready: as soon as it came out of the fire Mr Pulling ordered me to be ready to strike with a 14 pound sledge hammer. I told him *again* [Jimmy's emphasis] I knew nothing about such work. He requested me not to be *too* stubborn. To satisfy him I gave him a few blows. When he was quite satisfied I had told him the truth he not perceiving the cheat [i.e. he knew I had not cheated him] and on that account he would not turn me into government employ, but said I must do the best I could for him about the house.

Jimmy, in his new role as house help, continued to work for the kindly Mr Pulling. What follows is Jimmy's version of events, and large chunks of it have to be taken with a pinch of salt. In Jimmy's telling, his master's business failed, and Mr Pulling now found himself 'much reduced'. Jimmy decided to help out. 'I thought I ought to assist him in return for his kindness to me, for I was very sorry to see his children in want,' Jimmy writes, adding: 'I could not get what I wanted [i.e. money to help the Pulling family] by labouring, as I had no trade, but

I was determined to obtain it by fair or foul means, for my poor master had taken it so much to heart that he appeared deranged.' So, dear reader, please accept that Jimmy did what he did only to help the impoverished Mr Pulling and family. At least, that's what he says.

> In the evening I took a small dinghy out of the creek, watched my opportunity, and got alongside the barque *Bengal Merchant*. I soon made my way to the cabins and brought away a bag of 300 sovereigns besides a quantity of loose silver, which I put into my pockets. Returning on deck (it being dark) I met a man, which proved to be the steward. He was so much astonished that he gave me an opportunity of pushing him down on the deck before he could give the alarm.

The dinghy had drifted off, so Jimmy simply dived into the water clutching his spoils. Despite being weighed down with money, he managed to swim to a buoy and clung to it until the hue and cry had died down. He somehow made his way ashore. A bedraggled Jimmy returned to the Pulling household. It happened that Mr Pulling was away on business, and in his absence Jimmy told Mrs Pulling the true story and swore her to secrecy. The next day he went to several shops and bought supplies for the household, enough to keep them going for six months. He also handed over some money to Mrs Pulling. Then he asked her to turn him in to the Government Service[2]

---

2   The branch of government tasked with administering 'assignment'.

without telling them about the crime, ending his assignment with the Pullings.

When he arrived at the government barracks, he discovered to his horror that there was a £100 reward and a free pardon for any convict who could give information about the robbery. Then Mr Pulling returned home to discover his changed circumstances, and demanded to know from his wife what had happened. She told him Jimmy had bought the supplies, and had asked to be returned to government service. Mr Pulling jumped to the conclusion that Jimmy was up to no good with his wife, and simultaneously worked out for himself that Jimmy's generosity must have been at somebody else's expense. Jimmy was arrested, and charged with robbing the barque. This, of course, was a hanging offence. However, Jimmy again dodged the hangman. He did not have anything in his possession to connect him to the robbery, and both the captain and the steward of the *Bengal Merchant* failed to identify him. Jimmy explained to the magistrate ('a feeling gentleman, rare to be found in these Colonies') that he had bought the Pullings' supplies with money he had saved up. The result was too good to be true: acquitted, and with Mr Pulling gently rebuked by the magistrate for his ingratitude and unwarranted suspicions of this fine young man. That's Jimmy's story. As we shall now see, it might all be total fantasy.

━━ ━ ━ ━

In his journals, Jimmy is inclined to omit a few indiscretions, which are however painstakingly recorded in his convict conduct record. He arrived in Hobart Town in January 1824. On 22 April 1824 he was charged with stealing a cask[3] of butter and with having no lodgings. He was acquitted on both charges. It may well be that the Pulling story recounted above is a self-aggrandising fantasy version of that event, and the reality was much more prosaic: instead of acting like a seagoing Robin Hood and stealing money to help his master, he simply stole a cask of butter and got away with it. His record contains no mention of a charge of stealing money from a ship, nor of his acquittal on that charge.

A month later, on 22 May, Jimmy was charged with absconding and sentenced to 100 lashes. This crime and subsequent punishment are omitted from his two journals, and it would be understandable if the memory was too painful and humiliating for him to include it. We know from his conduct record that he stayed out of trouble until 31 August 1826, so what follows probably took place between May 1824 and August 1826 (if it happened at all).

According to his Norfolk Island journal, in his new guise as model convict and kindly benefactor, Jimmy was quickly assigned as a 'pulling hand' (oarsman) in the governor's barge, and moved on from that to coxswain of the government secretary's gig, a fast, light rowboat. In Jimmy's words: 'All things went well for a few months.' But Jimmy was not destined for

---

3   The word 'cask' can allude to a unit of volume rather than a physical barrel. There are various sizes of cask, ranging from 4.5 to 240 imperial gallons. A 'cask of butter' would very likely have been smaller than 240 gallons, which would have been beyond one man's ability to carry.

a peaceful life. The new governor, George Arthur, ordered a whaleboat to take some dispatches to Maria Island, about 58 miles (93 kilometres) by sea from Hobart, off the east coast of Van Diemen's Land. Arthur's regular coxswain was engaged elsewhere, so it fell to Jimmy to take charge of the boat.

Jimmy and his party were issued with muskets and cutlasses in case they were attacked. Jimmy even had a blunderbuss[4] loaned to him by Captain Walsh, the Superintendent of Government Craft. The weapons were soon needed. Their best route involved manhandling the whaleboat across a neck of land about a mile wide. They were about two-thirds of the way across when a group of Aboriginal men attacked them with a shower of spears, wounding one of Jimmy's crew. The attackers were driven off with pistols and muskets. Jimmy was now a man short, with some 500 metres of land remaining to haul across. With great difficulty, they reached the water with the whaleboat. Before they could launch it, a fresh shower of spears instantly killed the bow hand. Staying out of range of the spears meant braving dangerous surf. The men made it, though the whaleboat filled with gallons of water in the process.

The return journey was equally hazardous, with more attacks. They arrived back in Hobart Town to something of a hero's welcome. At this high point, Jimmy's gift for snatching defeat from the jaws of victory did not desert him.

---

4   A short-barrelled, muzzle-loading musket with a flared barrel for easy loading and quick (if inaccurate) firing.

I took the dispatches to Governor Arthur. The boat's crew were ordered ticket-of-leave after six months good conduct. I got charge of the *Rambler* cutter of 48 tons, and gave every satisfaction. I was earning plenty of money, not being addicted to drinking. Some scoundrels gave information that I was going to take away the cutter. This caused the first suspicion of my character and the cause of my misery. I was not looked upon as a person trustworthy, therefore I was determined to make my escape from the colony as soon as I could get a chance.

From this point, it is hard to reconcile Jimmy's accounts in his two journals with the official record. Let's start with Jimmy's version of events. His first attempt at escape ended in failure. With a fellow convict, Thomas Rush, he stole a whaleboat and set off to meet up with the brig *Elizabeth* anchored at Bricks Bay,[5] about 8 miles (13 kilometres) south of Hobart Town. The two escapees made it as far as the brig, and were accepted on board. The brig was about to sail for Macquarie Island, looking for seal oil. Macquarie Island is a bleak lump of rock about 1000 miles (1600 kilometres) south-east of Tasmania in the wild Antarctic Ocean, so the journey was arduous and dangerous. However, neither Jimmy nor the *Elizabeth* made it to the wild water. On the first night, bad weather forced the brig

---

5 Probably the bay at the mouth of the Browns River near the present town of Kingston, on the west bank of the Derwent Estuary. Convict brickmaking took place here in the early days of the settlement.

to take shelter close to shore, and this proximity to land—and therefore authority—changed the mood on board. Jimmy was taken prisoner, handed over to the authorities, and charged with stealing the whaleboat. That's Jimmy's version.

This is not what the official record tells us. According to his conduct record, on 28 August 1826 Jimmy absconded from Hobart Town and was found aboard the ship *Sydney Packet* (not the *Elizabeth*) off Bruny Island (note, no mention of Bricks Bay) 'with intent to escape from the colony'.

Back to Jimmy's version. His previous adventures and good behaviour now stood him in good stead. Captain Walsh, the Superintendent of Government Craft who had loaned him the blunderbuss, gave evidence of Jimmy's good character. Again he was acquitted, and a few days later found himself in charge of a 25-ton schooner. The official version is both more terse and more brutally credible: found guilty of absconding, sentenced to 50 lashes and six months on the chain gang. Rush received the same sentence.

There were more indiscretions to come. According to his conduct record, on 26 January 1827 he was charged with robbing one of the crew of the convict ship *Sir Charles Forbes*. This charge was 'dismissed for want of evidence'. On 16 March 1827 he was charged with 'being out all night'. Sentence: reprimanded. On 24 July 1827 he was accused of being 'out after hours and abusive and insolent to Private Henry Kelly of the 40th Regiment, then on duty at the Bonded Stores'. Again, reprimanded. On 10 June 1828 he was charged with 'making use of the Government Boat to his own private advantage, contrary to orders', and with 'taking men down the river without proper authority'. Sentence: 25 lashes.

None of this is recorded in either of Jimmy's journals. By Jimmy's account, his original escape attempt and its aftermath marked a turning point in his fortunes. He says he had been placed in charge of a 25-ton schooner, with two other crewmen. Jimmy can tell the story:

One of the hands being nearly free stole some pine plank to make himself a sea chest and took it on board without my knowledge. I was on shore at the time. He was taken to gaol for it, and me, having charge of the schooner, I was apprehended. The man only wanted ten days to do out of fourteen years. He was nearly broken-hearted and asked if there was any chance of his being saved. I said none, except for me to take it on myself. I consented to get convicted if he would promise to have the whaleboat ready when I got sent to a chain gang, for me to abscond with. He promised he would. I consented, acquitted him, and convicted myself by acknowledging to the planks. I got seven years transportation.[6] I was not downcast at this for I depended on the whaleboat. I went to the chain gang and one of the most dreadful places I have ever seen. I preferred death to remaining there three years. And the ungrateful wretch whom I thus sacrificed myself for

---

6   This was hardly a harsh outcome—he was already serving a sentence of transportation for life. However, the new sentence included three years on a chain gang, so it was definitely a step in the wrong direction.

never came near me. I was determined to escape from this scene of wretchedness or perish in the attempt.

Here the official record and Jimmy's version of events begin to converge. According to Jimmy's conduct record, on 19 November 1828 he was tried for stealing 70 boards (planks) valued at £2, the property of the King. Sentence: seven years' transportation. A bit over a year later, while labouring in irons on a government work gang in Hobart, he made a run for it. He managed to survive at large for a bit over a week, including three days in the bush without food, but was eventually caught, dragged back to Hobart Gaol and charged with 'feloniously absconding from the Chain Gang when under sentence of the Supreme Court'. This was a serious charge, with dire penalties if he was convicted. His conduct record gives the date of his first court appearance as 7 January 1830. At this hearing, he was remanded in custody for a week. The full trial took place on 30 January. This time there was no acquittal. Sentence: death. It was his second appointment with the hangman.

━━ ▭ ━━

The details that follow are probably fantasy—the commuting of a death sentence with only minutes to spare is more the stuff of fiction than fact. But Jimmy is a good storyteller, so here is his version:

The humane Captain Walsh again interceded for me and saved my life, though I was not acquainted with it until morning. I was pinioned [had my hands tied behind my back] and going out to be executed. I was then conveyed aboard the brig *Prince Leopold* for Macquarie Harbour.

At the very last minute, his death sentence was commuted to seven years' 'retransportation'. To Sarah Island.

Chapter 5

SARAH ISLAND

The all-pervading cruelty of the Sarah Island penal settlement is graphically illustrated by the fate of a convict named John Ollery. He had arrived in Van Diemen's Land in July 1819 aboard the convict ship *Coromandel*. His conduct record shows that, while he was no model prisoner, he was generally well behaved. On 22 January 1821 he was sentenced to 25 lashes for 'neglect of duty and [being] absent from muster'. Four days later, he was again accused of 'neglect of duty' and was sentenced 'to labour the same as the Gaol Gang for one week'. These were comparatively minor offences, and the sentence for the first offence was severe. On 19 January 1822 he was tried in Hobart for a much more serious crime, namely stealing cash from a Mr Thomas Stocker. He was sentenced 'to work in Irons at Macquarie Harbour for three years'.

He was transported to Sarah Island. There, on 27 April 1822, he was sentenced to 25 lashes for 'disobeying orders and refusing to work'. According to his conduct report, he received ten lashes only—'the Assistant Surgeon being of the opinion he could not bear the remainder'. Anywhere else but Macquarie Harbour, the authorities might have taken this as a warning of his frailty.

Ollery had been in generally poor health, and about a month after the interrupted flogging, he took himself off to the hospital on Sarah Island to report that he was unwell. As a result, he was accused of malingering, brought before the superintendent, and sentenced to 50 lashes. He was tied to the triangle to receive his punishment. According to an eyewitness, he 'pleaded very hard to be forgiven on the score of illness but it was all to no purpose'.

He was tied up and the punishment went on amidst the most heart-rending screams and cries for mercy, but his appeals were made to men that never forgave a lash. After 30 lashes he never spoke. When he received five more the Superintendent returned to submissively observe that he thought the man had fainted. The doctor then stepped off the gangway and found that he was quite dead. No one knew. The murmurs among the men say that he received five lashes after his death, but the affair ended without a question being asked.

Ollery's ordeal had lasted two hours. The official report of his death said he died in hospital five days later, probably of heart failure. He was buried in an unmarked grave on Hallidays Island, an uninhabited tree-covered rock just under a mile south of Sarah Island. Afterwards the island was known among the convicts as Ollery's 'Olidays.

The first superintendent of Sarah Island was a sadistic bully. Lieutenant John Cuthbertson of the 48th Northamptonshire Regiment had extraordinary powers: because the penal settlement was so far away from legal niceties like courts and lawyers, he was judge and jury, manager and magistrate, with the authority to dispatch summary justice. In this he was supported by the soldiers of the 48th Regiment, known as the Steelbacks. The name was not, as might be imagined, a tribute to their unflinching military heroism. It arose because they had been individually flogged so often that their backs were largely impervious to pain, and they didn't react to the cat-o'-nine-tails. Having been regularly flogged themselves, they saw no reason to treat the convicts with anything other than the same contempt and viciousness.

A graphic description of the mood of the island under Cuthbertson comes from the pen of an anonymous clerk in the commissariat in Hobart. The clerk, known only by the initials G.K., made eleven visits to Macquarie Harbour and Sarah Island between 1822 and 1832.[7] This is an extract from his account of his second voyage, in December 1823.

> I promised myself I would never return to Macquarie Harbour and Sarah Island. The violence of the place had invaded my sleep; John Ollery did not rest peacefully in my dreams. What I find on arrival is a filthy outpost of

---

7   G.K.'s recollections have been superbly edited by Richard Innes Davey and published in book form as *The Sarah Island Conspiracies*. G.K. made eleven actual voyages. As we shall see, the twelfth 'voyage' played a key role in the events that follow.

lost souls, living in the kind of squalor one might expect among the most benighted of savages. I have never experienced such misery and anger and sullen hatred as I find among these outcasts . . . welling up from some dark region of their souls. The men themselves are scarcely capable of mutiny: many are desperately ill. From the Hobart Store we have sent down what we thought to be adequate clothing or cloth, foodstuffs, medicinals, enough to maintain good health. But the length of the voyages, the lack of proper storage in such conditions, outright theft by military and prisoner—not to mention the officers and civilians of all ranks—and the severity of the climate have all conspired against them. Dysentery, rheumatics, malnutrition, scurvy, and all manner of infections of the lungs have reduced these men to pitiable wrecks. Those that are capable have taken to the woods in threes and fours to avoid the senseless violence of the military, only to be forced to return by cold and hunger, and have to endure the heavy penalties for absconding. Others have not returned and are presumed to have perished.

The superintendent had five punishments available to him, and Cuthbertson dispensed them daily and liberally: he could order a flogging; he could order the prisoner to work in irons; he could commit a convict to solitary confinement; he could deprive the convict of food, by ordering that he continue to work but on a diet of bread and water, or a diet without meat and therefore without protein; or he could order a demotion from any position of privilege. For major offences such as murder, a convict would be sent to Hobart for trial.

Flogging was Cuthbertson's regular response to convict misdemeanours. 'Disrespectful conduct': 50 lashes. 'Disobedience of orders and refusal to work': 50 lashes. On 23 April 1823 he sentenced no fewer than 31 prisoners to 25 lashes each for 'not assisting to apprehend 7 prisoners in the act of absconding'. In July of the same year, fifteen convicts received a total of 1700 lashes in the space of six days. The whole punishment process lasted more than seventeen hours.

The cruelty of the floggings is beyond belief. They were carried out with a particularly vicious version of the cat-o'-nine-tails whip known as a thief's cat. The Macquarie Harbour version was an enhanced design: heavier and larger than the 'cats' used in the army or navy. Each of the nine double strands of whipcord had at least seven knots tied in it, and the knots were reinforced with wax or even wire to inflict maximum pain and damage. An offending prisoner would have his back bared. Then he would be tied to a wooden tripod, known as a triangle, with his wrists bound to the apex. His legs would be splayed, and his ankles tied to the tripod's legs. With the victim bound and powerless, the flogging could begin. By the third or fourth stroke the victim's back would be a mass of blood. By the fiftieth stroke all skin would have been cut away, and the wounds would extend to his neck and arms. It was not uncommon for enough flesh to be peeled away during a flogging to expose the bone beneath. In the twelve years of the Sarah Island settlement, between 1822 and 1833, 1335 convicts received a total of 53,700 strokes of the lash, an average of 40 lashes per sentence.

Cuthbertson added a piece of preening sadism of his own. The triangles on Sarah Island were sited near the edge of the water, and Cuthbertson had a boardwalk constructed alongside, with the triangles near the halfway point and at a right angle to the boardwalk. Army officers wore tight white breeches tucked into polished boots, topped by a tailored crimson coat with plenty of gold and glitter on the collar and cuffs, and a plumed hat, all designed to impress. Cuthbertson turned up to the floggings in full regalia. The rules required that a flogging be witnessed by a doctor, to ensure that it was carried out lawfully; Cuthbertson devised a ritual walk, accompanied by the assistant surgeon Henry Crockett, to control the pace of the flogging.

The sound of his boots on the boards was the metronome. Cuthbertson and the doctor would walk together to one end of the boardwalk, pause, and turn. That was the signal to the flogger to strike. The perpendicular arrangement of board-walk and triangle meant that from one end of the boardwalk Cuthbertson could see the prisoner's back, and from the other end he could see his face. So the ghastly ritual continued . . . *thud, thud, thud, thud* of the polished boots on the boardwalk, pause, turn to watch, *WHACK. Thud, thud, thud, thud,* pause, turn, *WHACK.* At this pace it might take as long as an hour to deliver 50 lashes.

Crockett had the authority to halt a flogging if he thought the prisoner could take no more. According to the meticulous records kept on Sarah Island, in the course of 1268 floggings he witnessed, the surgeon intervened to halt only ten of them.

———

The daily routine on Sarah Island was inflexible. Here is an extract from regulations affecting convicts, issued on 6 July 1824.

At daylight every morning (Sundays excepted) a Boat proceeds to the Small Island to bring off the bad Characters who are kept there. The Bell then rings for Muster ½ an hour before Sunrise, when every Prisoner attends in the presence of the Superintendent.

They are then divided into Gangs and marched to the Pier, where they are rigidly searched to prevent Provisions, Knives, Fish Hooks etc etc from being taken away.

A quarter of an hour before Sunrise they are embarked in Boats and proceed to the Main [mainland], where they labour at the Farm, felling, rolling and brickmaking, and do not return until Sunset.

At one p.m. on Saturday, Prisoners are exempted from Labour in order that they may mend their Clothes.

At 8 p.m. every evening Prisoners are mustered in the Penitentiary in the presence of the Superintendent, who locks them up in their several Rooms, leaving 1 or 2 Constables in each.

On Sundays, the Church Service is read by the Assistant Colonial Surgeon, in the presence of the Commandant and all the prisoners.

There was a total ban on alcohol and tobacco for prisoners, although a steady black market in both was largely organised by the military. Food was always scarce, particularly as the farm was generally a failure. According to an 1827 report, the daily rations allocated to each convict were: 1 pound 4 ounces (570 grams) of wheatmeal; 1 pound (450 grams) of fresh meat or salt beef, or 10 ounces (280 grams) of salt pork; and 11½ ounces (325 grams) of salt. That was it. The rations were issued once a week in bulk, and it was up to the prisoner to preserve his allocation, prepare his own meals, and make the rations last the full week. Fresh vegetables were added when available, but that was not nearly often enough. Scurvy was a constant problem.

In 1824, the sadistic Lieutenant Cuthbertson came to a suitably sticky end. The schooner *Governor Sorell* was inside Macquarie Harbour when it broke loose from its mooring in a storm. It looked as though the ship would drift onto rocks and be lost forever. Cuthbertson led a rescue party, ordering a small boat out into the storm. The *Governor Sorell* obliged the rescuers by drifting onto a beach, where it could come to no further harm. The rescuers turned for home, into the teeth of the storm. Cuthbertson was a soldier, not a sailor, and he did not understand that facing into the wind and waves was the safest option for his tiny vessel. Instead he ordered his helmsman to turn around, away from the wind. The helmsman told him they risked being swamped if they began a turn that would put them side-on to the storm, but Cuthbertson would have none of it. The boat duly overturned. The helmsman grabbed an oar and used it as a float, allowing the wind to blow him to safety. Cuthbertson ordered the rest of the crew to stay with the upturned boat. They all drowned, including Cuthbertson. It was whispered afterwards that Cuthbertson might have been rescued, but nobody could be bothered.

It made little difference. The flogging triangles stayed busy.

———

Some convicts took an extraordinary path to death, which they saw as preferable to the tormented life of Sarah Island. On the night of 27 October 1827, a group of convicts on Small Island overpowered Constable George Rex. They captured three more prisoners—two convicts and a junior constable, Robert Grew— to act as witnesses to what followed. All four were bound and gagged and dragged down to the beach. The group then captured two more convicts and bound and gagged them, too. In the morning, they untied Rex, leaving his gag in place, led him down to the water and drowned him, making sure the bound and gagged others could see what was happening. The prisoners then summoned the soldiers and gave themselves up. In all, nine convicts were tried in Hobart for the murder of Constable Rex, and hanged. That was their escape plan successfully implemented. As a bonus, the witnesses had a nice trip to Hobart for their day in court, which meant a welcome break from Sarah Island.

It is fair to say that escape was uppermost in the minds of most of the convicts at Macquarie Harbour. Prisoners regularly absconded, either alone or in groups, but it seldom ended well.

The most notorious escapee was one Alexander Pearce, who absconded with seven others on 20 September 1822. They set off for Hobart Town by land, which would involve a 300-kilometre hike across high mountains and through dense, trackless forest. After eight days, three of the fleeing convicts had had enough and turned back to Macquarie Harbour, preferring punishment to starvation. It turned out to be a good call. The remaining five pushed on. After fifteen days their supplies ran out. However, Pearce astonished everyone by making it alone to the east coast of Van Diemen's Land. He rested up briefly in the countryside with some bushrangers, before being captured and taken to Hobart, his intended destination. In Hobart he confessed he had survived in the bush by eating his fellow escapees. A legal loophole meant he could not be tried in Hobart for murder, so he was simply returned to Sarah Island. He escaped again on 16 November 1823 with another convict, Thomas Cox, but was captured again within ten days. This time there was no loophole to save him. On 19 July 1824 he was tried for murdering and cannibalising Thomas Cox, and hanged in Hobart.

Another important escapee was Matthew Brady. He had assumed leadership of a convict rebellion at Macquarie Harbour in June 1824. On 7 June he escaped with thirteen others. He fled by sea before melting into the bush, and set himself up as the leader of a ragtag guerrilla army. The authorities were profoundly perturbed—they thought Brady and his men might attract more followers, which could lead to a general uprising. Indeed, that was what the prisoners at Macquarie Harbour hoped. There were endless rumours that Brady would shortly be arriving with his army, who would put the soldiers to flight and free the prisoners. Superintendent Wright, Cuthbertson's successor, even asked for extra soldiers to fight off an expected assault by Brady's men. The assault never happened. Instead, Brady and his gang abandoned their guerrilla ambitions and settled down to the steady work of bushranging. At one point, Governor Arthur offered a reward for information leading to Brady's capture. In response, Brady offered a reward of 20 gallons (230 litres) of rum to anybody who could deliver Governor Arthur to him. As so often with dreams of salvation, it all ended badly. After 22 months on the run—a long time in the life of a bushranger—Brady was captured, and on 4 May 1826 he was hanged in Hobart Gaol. Of the fourteen original escapees, twelve were hanged. When news of Brady's fate reached Macquarie Harbour, there was despondency among the convicts. Clearly the guerrilla army would not be coming to their rescue. So, while escape from Macquarie Harbour remained every convict's dream, the odds against success were dauntingly high.

———

The intention had always been to make the Macquarie Harbour settlement self-sufficient. This never really worked. The forested land around the harbour needed backbreaking work to clear it by hand before it could be planted with crops. Then the results were disappointing: the land was rocky, and such soil as there was proved to be acidic. Wheat failed. Potatoes were more successful, but they were regularly stolen and attempts to fence them off proved ineffectual. A few pigs survived and even flourished, but the settlement never managed to grow enough food to feed itself, let alone export food to Hobart or Sydney.

Timber proved to be a better bet. The local Huon pines were much in demand, and sold for good prices when they could be shipped out. The trees were huge—some of them had been there since Julius Caesar was a lad—and rolling them down to the river or harbour was supremely hard work, as well as being dangerous. It was especially difficult for the large numbers of men wearing irons.

Timber felling was often assigned as a kind of further punishment for men who had already been sentenced to work in chains. The convicts were called on to move the felled trees, weighing anything up to 12 tons each, using only handspikes, a block and tackle and their brute strength. The logs were rolled along makeshift tracks built from trees, sometimes over distances of up to a mile. When the logs reached the river they were rolled into the water, then lashed together to form rafts. The lashing was done by convicts, usually in chains and standing up to their waists in the icy water. The rafts were then towed down the harbour by a team of launches operated by convict oarsmen.

Overseers were capable of singling out a convict in chains for 'neglect of work', knocking him to the ground with a handspike and thumping him with a stick while he lay there, then reporting him for insolence and thereby earning him 50 lashes. Because food might be used to aid an escape, prisoners in work parties were forbidden to bring supplies of any kind with them. Convicts on timber-cutting duty worked all day without a meal. Before they set off they were thoroughly searched to make sure they were not carrying provisions, knives, even fish hooks—anything an absconding convict might use to provide himself with food.

The very remoteness of Macquarie Harbour, which made it appealing as a virtually escape-proof holding pen for convicts, worked against it as a trading base. Timber needed to be shipped to Hobart before it could be marketed, and that meant a hazardous 27-day journey in a ship small enough to clear the bar at the entrance to the harbour, but large enough to carry a useful load of timber. The shuttle of ships between Hobart and Macquarie Harbour was never satisfactory. If a ship ran late, there was no way to find out how or why it had been delayed. Had it been lost at sea? Who knew? Yet it might be carrying food that everybody at Macquarie Harbour needed for survival. All anyone could do was sit and wait.

This dismal regime continued from 1821 until 1825. There is unanimity in the various descriptions of the penal settlement. Eyewitnesses report a sullen, mutinous, embittered, sickly convict population, brutalised, subject to arbitrary and sadistic cruelty, routinely and calculatingly denied even the smallest of comforts or glimpses of humanity. It was an ill-disciplined, cowed, rancorous mess. Abandon hope, indeed.

Then things took a turn for the better.

Part 3

THE BRIG

Chapter 6

HOY

With the death by drowning of the unloved Lieutenant Cuthbertson, command of the settlement passed to another soldier, Lieutenant Samuel Wright. Like Cuthbertson, Wright came from the 48th 'Steelback' Regiment. He proved to be every bit as bad as his predecessor, without, it was said, Cuthbertson's one virtue, bravery. (Cuthbertson had fought with distinction in the Peninsular War of 1807–14 against Napoleon.) The brutal regime of daily floggings, occasional hangings, exhausting work, hunger, cold, disease and misery continued unchecked. Wright's command began in January 1824 and ended in April 1825. His replacement was something else altogether.

On 21 April 1825 Captain James Butler assumed command of the settlement. He came from a different regiment, the 40th Regiment of Foot, and had recently been promoted from lieutenant. The 40th had distinguished itself in the Peninsular War, and then played a key role in the Battle of Waterloo. In 1823 the regiment was assigned to the task of guarding convicts, on the transport ships and subsequently in New South Wales and Van Diemen's Land.

Although the 40th had been raised in the West Country of England (it was also known as the 2nd Somerset Regiment), Captain Butler came from an entirely different background. He was a Catholic, born in Dublin. That set him apart from the mainstream of the British Army: by law, Catholics could not be commissioned officers outside Ireland itself. The law was widely flouted, but it remained on the statute books. There were other problems. Public office holders had to take what was known as a 'sacramental test', designed to exclude Catholics and dissenters. They were required to swear an oath rejecting the doctrine of transubstantiation, a key Catholic belief that the communal bread and wine, after suitable blessing and prayers, are genuinely the body and blood of Christ. Without this commitment, Butler could not be sworn in as a magistrate, so he could not legally dole out punishments. The authorities decided to work around the oath-swearing problem by waiting until he had arrived at Macquarie Harbour and then appointing him a magistrate by letter. That spared everybody the embarrassment of a mendacious swearing-in ceremony.

Butler's reign hardly got off to an enlightened start. Realising that, until his formal appointment as a magistrate, any punishments he handed out were illegal, he simply sat on his hands for a month while awaiting developments. A few prisoners spent a few days in solitary confinement on his orders, but there were no formal trials, no witnesses were sworn in, and no floggings were ordered. The convict population could hardly be expected not to notice the sudden disappearance of the lash, and on 27 May they tested their luck by going on strike. A gang of twenty men downed tools and refused to work. Butler threatened them, to no avail. Finally one of the convicts shouted to the others that the commandant 'could not flog them but merely confine them', and confinement 'they could well bear'.

Butler snapped. He ordered the mutinous convict into his office, where he sentenced him to 25 lashes. Knowing what he was doing was illegal, he made a particular point of not swearing in witnesses or otherwise imitating court procedures This produced a profound effect: Butler had heard loud and clear that the convicts feared the lash more than they feared solitary confinement (one day's 'solitary' was generally regarded as the equivalent of five lashes). From that point onwards, he seldom used solitary confinement as a punishment. In his time as commandant he ordered no fewer than 612 floggings totalling 23,696 lashes, an average of 39 strokes per flogging. So he was clearly no dewy-eyed liberal.

However, Butler's arrival coincided with a subtle change in the attitude of the authorities towards their convict charges. What use were these convicts? people asked. The answer was obvious: they could work. And wasn't this a win–win? If the convicts could be trained to do much-needed and useful work, they might be kept out of mischief while actually redeeming themselves and contributing to society. Previously work had been mindless and at times pointless. Convicts were punished with a spell on the treadmill, grinding grain into flour. That was at least some use. At other times they were simply confined to a cell equipped with a handwheel and told to turn the wheel through a certain number of revolutions a day. The handwheels were connected to nothing, produced nothing, and served no useful purpose. The original Sarah Island regulations posted by Governor Arthur put it succinctly:

> Never lose sight of a continued, rigid, unrelaxing discipline; and you must find work and labour, if it consists only of opening up cavities and filling them up again. As far as possible do not lose sight of the importance of combining utility with labour, [but] hard labour is the main objective.

Unlike his unloved predecessors, and to his great credit, Butler began a program of improvement on Sarah Island. Solid buildings sprang up: a brick gaol (1826), a bakehouse and a solid stone penitentiary (both in 1828). Prisoners were no longer confined in leaking, drafty conditions. Thomas Lempriere, the settlement's commissariat officer, wrote: 'Captain Butler had, after recovering a considerable area from the sea, formed a spacious dockyard, fronted by substantial log-built quays, and protected from the north-west gales by a high lath fence.'

The clerk G.K., who wrote so touchingly about his voyages to Macquarie Harbour, was sceptical. He wrote:

> I hold out no great hope that Butler will succeed in his plan to make the Settlement a place of reformation, for all his

energy and his determined character. He is a Benthamite:[1] despite the regular floggings he orders he believes they have no good effect and he seems keen to construct a prison along the lines that Jeremy Bentham has promoted in the tracts that Captain Butler thrusts upon all and sundry.

G.K.'s understandable doubts proved to be ill-founded. Butler's new regime succeeded. Little industries sprang up on Sarah Island, offering the convicts genuine work. These included tanning, shoemaking and brickmaking. As the convicts' lives steadily improved, so did morale and discipline. The soldiers and supervisors were forced to acknowledge that men who had just been flogged couldn't and wouldn't work effectively. Something had to change, and it did: as morale improved, floggings fell by some 90 per cent, as did other, less draconian punishments. Those who worked on the gangs were offered extra rations.[2] Morale soared higher.

As we have already seen, the sea journey between Hobart and Sarah Island was no picnic. Right from the earliest days of the settlement, one of the tasks required of convicts, along with clearing the land and constructing buildings, was to repair ships

---

1 A follower of Jeremy Bentham, the English prison reformer.

2 The July 1827 list of those awarded extra rations makes for extraordinary reading. As well as various shipwrights, carpenters, constables and boat crews, extra rations were awarded to convict John Flynn, whose 'designation or employment' is given as 'flagellator'. He was the colony's flogger.

that had been damaged on the voyage. So the convicts built a slipway to allow ships to be dragged out of the water for repairs. At some point there must have been a light-bulb moment when somebody realised the blindingly obvious: given that the timber being felled on the banks of the Gordon River was intended for shipbuilding, and given the difficulty of transporting the heavy logs in light ships across the bar at the entrance to Macquarie Harbour, *why not build the ships on Sarah Island instead?* That would provide useful work for the convicts, and at the same time solve the problem of transporting the logs, which would instead be sawn up and hewn on Sarah Island before being converted into sturdy ships.

According to Tasmanian government archives, the first major ship constructed on Sarah Island was a 35-ton two-mast schooner called the *Governor Sorell*, which later played a central role in the death of Commandant Cuthbertson. The records show that the ship was completed in February 1824, over a year before the arrival of Captain Butler. The next major ship was the *James Lucas*, a sloop-rigged lighter[3] of unknown tonnage, launched sometime in 1825. This time we have the name of the supervising shipbuilder, a convict named Newton Gray.

The official records tell a contradictory story. They show that a convict named Newton Gray arrived in Tasmania in 1823 on the ship *Asia* (the same ship that brought Jimmy Porter to Hobart). The ship's records show that he had been convicted

---

3   In non-nautical language, a flat-bottomed, one-masted sailing ship used to transport small loads in shallow water.

at Durham and Sadberge Assizes on what looks like 6 March 1823. According to his conduct record, Gray had been sentenced to transportation for life for 'breach of contract'. There is no reference to any new offence committed in Hobart that might have led to his 'retransportation' to Sarah Island, so it is difficult to work out how or why he got there. His conduct record says he was granted a conditional pardon on 25 November 1829. He was charged again with breach of contract on 12 April 1830, but he seems to have been released after promising to do the work for which he had signed up. So far, so good.

However, other historians point to a shipbuilding convict called Austen Gray, also sentenced to transportation for life at Durham and Sadberge Assizes and sent to Van Diemen's Land in 1823 aboard the *Asia*. The same sources say this Gray was a convicted highwayman, which makes more sense of the sentence of transportation for life, which would be pretty stiff for the white-collar crime of 'breach of contract'. To add to the confusion, the official records show no trace of a convict called 'Austen Gray', while G.K. refers to Newton Gray as a 'highwayman'.

Whatever the facts, Newton Gray was the first named ship-builder on Sarah Island. After the launch of the *James Lucas* in 1825, he is credited with overseeing the construction of the two-masted schooner *Despatch*, launched in December 1825. The *Despatch* seems to have lasted a mere four months. It went missing in March 1826 on the short trip from Hobart to Maria Island, and was never heard of again. Meanwhile, his first ship, *James Lucas*, was wrecked off Bruny Island in May 1829.

By 1827 a new shipbuilding name had entered the lists, that of Thomas Cole. Unlike Gray, Cole was not a convict but a civilian officer who arrived at Macquarie Harbour with his wife and large family. He was given the title of master shipbuilder, but he seems to have been no more competent than Gray. His first ship, the *Derwent*, a two-masted brig of 81 tons, went into government service sometime around May 1827 and appears to have been abandoned ('hulked') by the government in 1831. His second ship, the *Opossum*, a one-masted cutter, was started by him and completed by Newton Gray in October 1827. It might be that the blame for the demise of the *James Lucas*, *Despatch* and *Derwent* should lie squarely with their captains and crew and not with the builders, Gray and Cole. Not so the *Opossum*. A survey report said of it: 'Unsafe when laden, can carry but a small cargo, sails very indifferently and will not work but in smooth water.' To be fair, the *Opossum* survived longer than its predecessors. It was not wrecked until 1853.

What of the first major ship built at Sarah Island, the *Governor Sorell*, you might well ask? Answer: wrecked in October 1827 at Hope Beach, not far from Hobart. So shipbuilding got off to a shaky start at Sarah Island. Then David Hoy arrived, and the shipbuilding business was transformed out of sight.

———

David Hoy is a difficult man to pin down. We know he was a Scot, that he was born in 1792, and that he died a very wealthy man in Hobart in 1862. Given his contribution to both convict reform and the Australian shipbuilding industry, his face ought to be familiar from banknotes, postage stamps and art gallery walls throughout the land. Instead the only likeness I could find of him is a pen-and-ink sketch of a man with a round face adorned by long sideburns and strong eyebrows, puffing on a small pipe, and with a pork-pie hat perched uneasily on his head. He was reputedly more than a little pleased with himself, to the point where the convicts referred to him as Old Hooey or, more respectfully, The Admiral.

He first learned the craft of shipbuilding in his native Scotland, then moved to Boston in the United States and worked in shipyards there. His American experience shaped his design ideas: the Boston shipbuilders were interested in only one thing—speed. If that meant the ship became hard to handle at sea, so be it. Speed was everything. While Hoy's designs were sound and had no difficulty passing surveys and inspections, ships' masters complained that they were a bit of a handful on the open ocean. No matter . . . they were fast.

Hoy had been aboard the American ship *Chesapeake* during the 1812–15 war between Britain and the United States. *Chesapeake* was captured by the British frigate *Shannon* on 1 June 1813 just outside Boston Harbor. We can take a pretty good guess at what happened next. The British were in the habit of telling any British seamen captured in this way that they had just joined the Royal Navy. So, after being nabbed aboard the *Chesapeake*, Hoy very likely spent the next few years as a Royal Navy sailor, at least until the end of the Napoleonic Wars in 1815.

What he did between his spell in the Royal Navy and his arrival in Hobart in 1824 is anybody's guess. He told others that he had been 'repatriated' to Scotland, where he presumably set about resuming his career as a shipbuilder. If that is what happened, then it is at least likely that he heard of the wonderful new shipbuilding timber Huon pine, and decided to set off to Van Diemen's Land to make full use of it. When he arrived in Hobart he discovered to his dismay that nobody wanted to employ him as a ship designer. Yet that was all he ever wanted to do—design and build his own ships.

As we've seen, the shipbuilding industry on Sarah Island was not exactly running smoothly. The combined efforts of Thomas Cole and Newton Gray were producing ships that were dismissed as 'unsafe when laden', while the trail of shipwrecks and other disasters involving the convict shipbuilders' output suggested that luck was not on the side of the Sarah Island construction team. It was clearly time for a new man with new ideas.

Like Cole, Hoy was a free man and not a convict. He was unmarried, with no family, so he would only be one extra mouth to feed. Cole had been afforded the title master shipbuilder from day one. The same courtesy was offered to Hoy. He arrived at Macquarie Harbour in October 1827 as the new master shipbuilder. The reform-minded Captain Butler was still commandant of the settlement, and Hoy set out to make the best of his new situation.

It is all too easy to say 'so what?' about Sarah Island shipbuilding. But there were serious problems to overcome, and old fears and paranoias to be assuaged. If the Huon pine logs were to be shaped and trimmed for use as ships' timbers, and if this work was to be carried out by convict labour, then that meant issuing convicts with heavy, sharp tools, which could be useful weapons if things turned ugly.

Hoy chose his workforce carefully. Obviously experience with ships was an advantage. So were intelligence, zeal and ingenuity. He wanted his workforce to be an elite, so he negotiated better conditions for them, including extra rations. So much did morale improve under Hoy's regime that one convict, James Reeves, who had completed his sentence and was a free man, asked if he could stay on at Sarah Island for a couple of months to complete two ships then under construction.

That perceptive chronicler G.K. had arrived at Sarah Island with Hoy on the same ship, *Prince Leopold*, in October 1827. He returned to the island a year later, and wrote:

Mr Hoy has settled in marvellously, and he and Newton Gray are a force to be reckoned with! The shipyards are complete and now in full operation. There is a sense of purpose there, even the pot boys and sweepers are cheerful, and one extraordinary thing, they seemed to be chanting as they worked, like nursery rhymes, some strange incantation, till I realized they were spelling the letters of their tools, the bricks and stones, the timber and rope and pitch were being spelled out, a matter of delight for Mr Schofield [the chaplain]. One of his first tasks was to establish the schoolhouse.

Each new boat laid and built and launched creates a wave of new interest throughout the Settlement: launch days for the larger ships become a kind of holiday for all. The work in the yards continues long after muster, the extra gangs made up of volunteers and those few of the military who find such occupation preferable to the gambling games and hunting parties favoured by most of the regiments.

Clearly things had moved on dramatically since G.K. wrote about Sarah Island, in December 1823: 'I have never experienced such misery and anger and sullen hatred as I find among these outcasts.'

Hoy's record at Macquarie Harbour is astonishing. Cole and Gray had built 35 ships between 1824 and 1827, and most were light. Between 1829 and 1833 the Hoy shipyard built 96 ships, many of them large. (The brig *Tamar* was 134 tons.) Under Hoy's direction, Sarah Island became the biggest and busiest shipbuilding yard in Australia at that time.

———

The year 1829 saw two major events in the life of the settlement. The far-sighted James Butler was recalled as superintendent, and replaced by Captain James Briggs. To put it mildly, Briggs's appointment was not a step in the right direction. He was stuffy, dim, snobbish and a bit prickly. When, in a sermon, the chaplain William Schofield delivered a fairly regular Wesleyan call for humility, saying, 'Not many win, not many noble are called,' Briggs took this as an insult aimed at him. Relations between the chaplain and the superintendent remained frosty ever after. According to G.K., Briggs tried to restore the harsher discipline of earlier years: 'For a while, The Cat rules again, and the solitary confinement cells are filled.' Briggs was not popular, and his soldiers of the 63rd Regiment made no secret of their resentment at being posted to Macquarie Harbour. Although things did not revert to the worst days of Cuthbertson and Wright, there was no doubting that the arrival of Briggs and his 63rd Regiment was a turn for the worse.

The other major event originated three years earlier, in 1826, with the purchase by the government in Hobart of the brig *Cyprus*. The intention was to use the *Cyprus* to replace the supply vessel *Duke of York*, which shuttled between Hobart and Macquarie Harbour and leaked like a sieve.[4]

However, the *Cyprus*'s career as a supply vessel was cut short in August 1829. The brig was on its way from Hobart to Macquarie Harbour when bad weather forced it to shelter in Recherche Bay, on the southeast coast of Van Diemen's Land. While the ship was under way in the bad weather, several of the convicts had had their irons struck off to help operate the ship. In Recherche Bay, under the leadership of William Swallow, they mutinied and seized it. Fortunately for them, the *Cyprus* was carrying enough food and equipment to supply the Sarah Island settlement for weeks, so the rebels were well set up for a long voyage. They used the paint in the store to change the ship's name from *Cyprus* to *Edward*, and set off for New Zealand, then Japan, and finally China. They scuttled the *Cyprus* in the Pearl River near Canton.

---

4   The saga of the purchase of the *Cyprus*, and its major refit in the Sarah Island shipyard, is told in detail by G.K. in his account of his October 1827 voyage to Macquarie Harbour.

The affair had the colony agog. Ballads were written. Newspapers carried full accounts of the seizure and escape. There was no getting away from the gloating, triumphant tone of the articles. In the words of the ballad 'Cyprus Brig':

First we landed the soldiers, the captain and his crew.
We gave three cheers for Liberty and soon bid them adieu.
William Swallows he was chosen our commander for to be.
We gave three cheers for Liberty and boldly put to sea.

Play on your golden trumpets, boys, and sound your cheerful notes,
The Cyprus *brig's on the ocean, boys, by justice does she float.*

It was enough to give people ideas.

———

Jimmy Porter arrived at Macquarie Harbour sometime in early 1830, aboard the brig *Prince Leopold*. He says he was the only prisoner on the voyage, which had taken sixteen days in dreadful weather. Although by 1830 the Sarah Island settlement had improved out of all recognition from the dark days of Cuthbertson and Wright, Jimmy was not the sort of chap to miss an opportunity for a bit of self-pity. According to his journal, he was not impressed by what he saw on arrival, nor by those who greeted him. He was presumably brought before Captain Briggs. They did not hit it off.

I was landed and taken before the Commandant. I found him every thing but a gentleman—a complete Tyrant.

He ordered what clothes I had on to be burned and gave me a suit of yellow to be sent to work, and at night to be sent to an Island where there was upward of 200 of what he called *out and outers*—men who would strain every point to get away.

It was a most wretched place for the most common necessaries of comfort—hours before daybreak we were roused and a pint of thin miserable gruel was allowed each man. *Into the boats* was the word, and then we had to remain in a bleak wind and all weathers till daylight, when we were mustered, led to our work and getting nothing to eat until we again returned to the Island which would be very likely dark, wet through and not a spark of fire to dry our clothes before we were again drove out. Nothing but misery, flogging and starvation—murders were frequently committed, twice or three times a month,[5] with a view to ridding themselves of a wretched existence. Out of every 100 young men, 96 would have sore backs. In fact, so bad was the treatment that death was preferable.

Most of this complaining may well have been rooted in reality. After all, Sarah Island remained a penal settlement, not a holiday camp, or even a shipyard. But it is only fair to point out that Jimmy came too late for the worst of it, and in nice time to benefit from the best of it.

---

5   This is simply not true. Murders were comparatively rare.

Chapter 7

PLOT

Jimmy Porter does not go into much detail in his journals about his life on Sarah Island, other than to continue his complaints: 'I was labouring under this dreadful state of things for 12 months.' We know, bizarrely, that he had an excellent singing voice and sang in the choir set up by the chaplain William Schofield, so it seems likely that he at least put on a show of becoming a model prisoner. In fact, he seems to have stayed out of trouble for more than two years. He arrived on Sarah Island early in 1830, and his conduct record remained clean until 11 July 1832. Then he was accused of 'neglect of duty in not taking care of some Tobacco in his charge' and sentenced to 25 lashes. He resumed his pattern of good behaviour for the next four months. Then, on 7 November, he was charged with 'leaving his work contrary to Orders' and sentenced to three weeks on bread and water, later reduced to twelve days. He mentions none of these clashes with authority in either of his journals.

He had barely completed the last punishment when he was in much more serious trouble. On 18 December he was tried for 'absconding into the Woods on the 11th inst [11 December]'. In his Norfolk Island journal Jimmy gives a long and elaborate account of this escape. He names his fellow absconders as convicts James Sheedy and William Holt. As Jimmy tells it: 'We had to take to the mountains without a bit of food, being closely pursued, and we would rather famish than go back.' After less than a week of freedom, the three were captured and brought back to Sarah Island.

An altogether more light-hearted version of this story is given by the government clerk G.K. in his account of his eleventh and final sea voyage to Sarah Island. As they entered Macquarie Harbour via Hell's Gates, he writes, they picked up two new passengers, an escaped convict and his captor John Little. The convict was Jimmy Porter. He had been on the loose for four days.

The story of Jimmy's captor John Little is almost as interesting as Jimmy himself. John Little was neither a soldier nor a constable but a fellow convict sentenced to transportation for life to Sarah Island. He arrived in Van Diemen's Land aboard the *Caledonia* on 24 September 1819, having been sentenced to a mere seven years' transportation. His conduct record shows that he was in trouble most of the time. On 17 April 1827 his sentence was increased to transportation for life, and he was subsequently 'retransported' from Hobart to Sarah Island.

Little's status as a fellow convict probably explains the next development. According to G.K., 'the two of them came aboard, hard to tell which the hunter and which the hunted, laughing and joking together'. They behaved rather as two children might, victor and vanquished in a game of hide and seek. In G.K.'s version, Jimmy had absconded for a bet. If he could stay on the run for more than three days, he would win a month's spirits rations, a seriously valuable prize. Jimmy being Jimmy, he also arranged to take a slice of the side bets placed by the soldiers on the length of his time on the run, and in G.K.'s words, 'he stands to make a tidy sum on the exercise'.

Why did a fellow convict put an end to Jimmy's freedom? The answer can be found in John Little's convict conduct record. An entry reads: 'N.B.: a recommendation of this man by the Commandant of Macquarie Harbour for his conduct in the apprehension of Runaways ordered to be recorded on the books in his favour.'

G.K. reports that Jimmy expected to receive ten to twenty days' solitary confinement as punishment. However, to Jimmy's dismay, David Hoy was furious with him for absconding and insisted on a punishment of 25 lashes. As Hoy cheerfully pointed out to Jimmy: 'You'll be over the worst of that in a day or two and I can have you back at the yards instead of inside that ridiculous prison.'

The final outcome was a great deal more savage than Hoy's off-handed suggestion. In Jimmy's Norfolk Island journal, he reports that he and his two fellow escapees were each sentenced to 300 lashes, the sentence to be carried out 100 lashes at a time on three successive Mondays. However, again according to Jimmy, after the first 100 had been administered, the commandant changed his mind and ordered that the remaining 200 be administered the next day. This was done, leaving Jimmy and his two companions 'more dead than alive'.

The only thing wrong with this terrible tale is that it is almost certainly untrue. According to Jimmy's official conduct record, he was sentenced to 100 lashes, six months in chains and two years' gaol at night, for absconding. Two other convicts, James Sheedy and William Holt, were sentenced at Sarah Island on the same day for the same offence, and awarded the same punishment. Without in any way diminishing the severity of the sentence—100 lashes is a fearsome ordeal—the plain fact is that Jimmy, not for the first time, is exaggerating. Still, it is fair to say that by mid-December 1832 convict P324 did not have much to look forward to on Sarah Island.

As we have seen, George Arthur, the governor of Van Diemen's Land, was a believer in the civilising benefits of stern punishment. It was he who had decreed that there should be no comforts or rewards on Sarah Island, only zero tolerance and piled-on misery. By 1826, during the period of James Butler's command, Arthur became uneasy over rumours that the settlement had softened to the point where it might lose its capacity to terrorise the convict population.

The other concern was escape. When Sarah Island was established in 1822, it was so remote and cut off that escape seemed impossible. However, with the steady stream of free settlers arriving in the colony, not to mention convicts who had completed their sentence and were now free, the boundaries of the settled area of Van Diemen's Land had steadily expanded. There was a real danger that the 'free' areas would eventually get uncomfortably close to previously remote penal settlements, which would mean that escaping convicts would not have far to go to find civilisation. Furthermore, the convicts on Sarah Island had become adroit at slipping their leg-irons, which meant they could make a run for it into the bush with some chance of getting away.

As it was, the Macquarie Harbour settlement still presented all sorts of problems. It was both difficult and expensive to supply. The harbour entrance remained a hazard for ships. There were endless shortages of drinking water. The soil was poor and agriculture suffered as a result. Last but not least, Sarah Island could not hold more than about 500 prisoners. Yet convicts continued to arrive in the colony by the boatload from Britain. Arthur decided to look elsewhere, and finally settled on Port Arthur. A former timber station, Port Arthur was first settled in 1830. At 60 miles (97 kilometres) southeast of Hobart it was still remote, and its geography made escape difficult. The prison would be built just beyond a narrow neck of land with sea on both sides. Thick forest beyond the narrow neck would make any overland escape difficult. It had plenty of fresh water and promising agricultural land nearby. Arthur made his decision: Sarah Island was to be closed down, and its convict population moved to Port Arthur.

At first Port Arthur was used as a kind of halfway house between normal convict life and the harsh world of secondary penal settlements like Sarah Island. Some of the more favoured convicts on Sarah Island were moved early to Port Arthur to share some of their skills. Records show that as early as April 1831 the hospital at Port Arthur was staffed largely by former Sarah Island prisoners. Shipbuilders, carpenters and blacksmiths from Macquarie Harbour were relocated to Port Arthur, not only to continue their work but also to train Port Arthur prisoners. This naturally depleted the workforce and skill pool on Sarah Island.

The order to abandon the Macquarie Harbour settlement was issued by the British colonial secretary on 27 December 1832. It called on the commandant to 'make immediate preparatory arrangements for abandoning the Settlement at Macquarie Harbour, consequently no new works of any description should be commenced, *but any vessels now building will of course be completed*' (my emphasis).

By the end of 1833, Sarah Island and Macquarie Harbour had been more or less cleared of civilians, convicts and soldiers. The last official shipment of convicts sailed in October 1833. Ships under construction had been completed and had already been put into service. There was one ship not quite finished, a 140-ton brig to be named *Frederick*. The intention had been to finish the *Frederick* at Sarah Island, pack it with the settlement's remaining provisions, and sail it to Hobart. Ten convicts were chosen to remain behind: Jimmy Porter, John Barker, William Cheshire, John Dady, John Fair, John Jones, James Leslie, Charles Lyon, Benjamin Russen and William Shiers. They were a mix of sailors and shipyard workers. Jimmy was coxswain of the pilot boat and knew his way through the treacherous entrance to Macquarie Harbour. John Fair was a former ship's officer (he had been captain of the forecastle of a ship named *Genoa 74*). On arrival in Van Diemen's Land, John Barker had given his occupation as watchmaker. He prudently failed to mention that he was also a skilled gunsmith. All in all, the ten convicts had the makings of a competent crew.

David Hoy naturally remained behind to supervise the final days of construction. So did Charles Taw (a notorious drunk), who had been the civilian pilot guiding ships through the tricky Macquarie Harbour entrance, and who would captain the *Frederick* on its journey to Hobart. His crew would also include a steward (Nichols), a first mate (James Tait), plus the ten convicts. Finally, he would also have aboard a free man (McFarlane), who appears to have arrived at Sarah Island as a convict but who had served his sentence. Four soldiers stayed behind at Macquarie Harbour to act as guards both during the construction and during the voyage.

It was not Governor Arthur's wish. To his reported fury, he was forced to accept that, rather than empty Sarah Island totally and move everything to Port Arthur, a handful of convicts[6]

---

6 There is some confusion over the number of convicts who stayed behind: a contemporary account in the *Hobart Town Courier* puts the number at twelve, while most other reports give it as ten. The question of who was and who was not a convict comes down to whether two men, McFarlane and Nichols, were still serving a sentence at the time of the voyage or whether they were free men. The probability is that they were still convicts under sentence, but McFarlane may have been recently freed. He may therefore have felt no need to escape.

needed to remain behind to finish building the *Frederick* and help sail it to Hobart.

———————

At this point, it is probably worth looking in detail at the size and appearance of the *Frederick*. We know that in the language of the sea she 'drew' about 140 tons, which means that when afloat she displaced 140 tons of water. This sounds a lot until you consider that Sydney Harbour's famous Manly ferry draws 1122 tons, making it about eight times the size of *Frederick*. We also know that *Frederick* was a brig, with two masts of about equal size, and at least one of the masts (usually the slightly shorter foremast) square-rigged. The second main mast may have carried a mainsail and a foresail, or it may have been square-rigged also.

No contemporary drawings exist of the *Frederick*. The only representation available is an etching engraved in 1952 by the Australian artist Geoffrey Ingleton and titled *The Brig Frederick Departs from Sarah's Island, Macquarie Harbour, Van Diemen's Land*. The 114th of 150 prints from the etching is held by the National Library of Australia. The ship in the etching carries square-rigged sails on both masts. This predominance of square-rigging would have made the *Frederick* awkward to handle unless the wind was directly behind. The etching also shows a large gaff-rigged sail behind the main mast. For all the etching's considerable grace and attention to detail, it is scarcely an accurate historic record of the *Frederick*'s departure. For a start, the ship is under full sail whereas we know that winds were strong that day and that only two sails were 'flown'.

A brig was a formidable fighting ship. An armed brig might carry between ten and eighteen guns. Ships of the brig class were both fast and manoeuvrable, which made them the popular choice of pirates. So John Barker and his ragtag crew had the advantage of a well-designed and well-constructed wooden sailing ship which could, in theory, take them anywhere in the world. However, it was no holiday cruise ship. Accommodation would be cramped and uncomfortable, and the output from the galley, or kitchen, would be unlikely to trouble the Michelin inspectors.

———

It is not absolutely clear how and when the idea arose that the convicts might seize the *Frederick* and sail away to freedom. In one version, given by Jimmy Porter years later but prudently left out of his two journals, the idea had been hatched around the time construction began. The original plan was a mass escape, with 50 or 60 convicts, but the opportunity never arose. The ship was well behind its construction schedule, the weather was as bad as usual, and the window of opportunity never opened.

However, there is evidence of some astute forward planning. John Barker took surreptitious lessons in open-sea navigation from William Philips, a fellow Sarah Island convict who had been a fisherman in Cornwall and had sailed with the East India Company. Barker also used his gunsmith's skills to convert some old musket barrels into improvised pistols. As a result, the remaining convicts were armed. Making the pistols alone must have represented many weeks of skilled work, not to mention weeks of careful scrounging. Barker also thoughtfully provided the convicts with a makeshift tomahawk.

In all the planning, one key question must have been: once they'd commandeered the *Frederick*, where would they pilot it to? The convicts who took the *Cyprus* had finally chosen to head north, after a detour to New Zealand, and had finished up in China. Perhaps that was the best bet? At some point Jimmy must have piped up and said something to the effect that he had a wife and son in Chile, he could recommend it as somewhere not under the thumb of the British, and the winds between Van Diemen's Land and the South American coast were generally favourable, unlike the winds between Van Diemen's Land and China. Why not go there?

———

By 11 January 1834 the *Frederick*'s construction had advanced sufficiently for the brig to put to sea. At ten that morning the largely completed ship and its motley crew set off for the last time from Macquarie Harbour. There were sighs of relief all round. By dusk they had sailed a full 23 miles (37 kilometres), as far as the harbour entrance. There they anchored. Captain Taw ordered Jimmy Porter and William Cheshire to go ashore and bring back some potatoes from an abandoned farm. David Hoy and two soldiers went with them.

The convicts had agreed among themselves that if there was a chance (in Jimmy's words, 'a slant of wind') that the ship could be seized then and there, those still on board the *Frederick* were to go ahead. They would signal the convicts in the shore party that they had seized the ship by hoisting the ship's ensign flag upside down. In the event, there was no signal, and Jimmy and the rest of his party returned impassively to the ship.

The wind then picked up and swung around to the northwest, meaning it was blowing squarely into the harbour entrance and causing a heavy swell. Crossing the bar was difficult enough at the best of times. But sailing a 140-ton vessel through a passage only 70 metres wide straight into the wind, and into the teeth of a substantial swell, would be impossible. The *Frederick* remained at anchor near the harbour entrance for a day and two nights, waiting for the weather to improve. Then, rather than continue to toss about, Taw ordered the crew to up anchor and take shelter behind Wellington Head, about 2 miles (3 kilometres) away. So at about nine o'clock on the morning of 13 January the *Frederick* anchored for the last time in Macquarie Harbour, about 300 metres off Wellington Head. All remained quiet until the evening.

———

At this point it is only fair to warn the reader about the sheer difficulty of working out what actually happened in Macquarie Harbour that evening. The accounts in Porter's two journals were each written with diametrically opposed intentions. The journal written in Hobart was intended to sell the idea that Jimmy was a poor, misled, contrite dupe, more of a well-intentioned bystander than a scheming criminal. The Norfolk Island journal is an exercise in self-aggrandisement in which he portrays himself as ringleader and plotter-in-chief. Fortunately we also have the accounts of David Hoy and First Mate Tait of the *Frederick*. From these four accounts it is possible to piece together some kind of sensible narrative.

What seems clear from the various accounts and from subsequent events is that the convicts were determined to avoid violence. So bluff, stealth and subterfuge would have to be the order of the day. The most urgent task was to get the soldiers and McFarlane out of the way. Jimmy suggested to the sergeant and one of the soldiers that they might take the opportunity to do a little fishing while everybody waited for the weather to improve. They concurred. Captain Taw gave permission for them to take the whaleboat and try their luck. Jimmy then feigned a stomach cramp and remained behind. Jimmy's chosen sergeant and soldier plus McFarlane set off in the whaleboat, armed with hooks, lines and bait. Three down, two to go.

Jimmy decided that his irresistible singing voice would be the best hope of completing the task non-violently. He suggested to the two remaining soldiers that they might like to accompany him below decks to the forecastle (or fo'c'sle).[7] There he would treat them to a few beautifully rendered songs. The two soldiers agreed, but only one followed Jimmy below decks. The other remained on the deck, sitting on the windlass, the heavy winch used on sailing ships to raise the anchor. Three convicts— Benjamin Russen, James Leslie and William Cheshire—stayed on deck to keep an eye on him. The others went below to listen to Jimmy.

---

7 That part of the bow of the ship serving as sleeping quarters for the crew.

With only one soldier to charm, Jimmy launched into the song 'The Grand Conversation Under the Rose'.[8] This long and frankly turgid ballad was composed at the end of the Napoleonic Wars. From the British point of view it was slightly subversive, and therefore popular in immediate post-war austerity. It praised Napoleon, and lamented the sufferings of returning British soldiers, whose reward for risking their lives was poverty and indifference. It must have been literally music to the ears of the solitary soldier. At one point Jimmy struggled to remember the words, but William Shiers kindly prompted him, and the performance continued.

Then came the signal to strike. Benjamin Russen, one of the three convicts remaining on deck, stamped on the wooden floor above Jimmy and his six fellow convicts. Shiers immediately put an improvised pistol to the solitary soldier's head. In Jimmy's words: 'He was quiet directly.' Up on deck, James Leslie and his two fellow convicts now captured the heavily outnumbered second soldier.

Jimmy and Shiers rushed up the stairs and onto the deck, leaving the other five convicts below to guard their soldier. Once on deck, they sealed the hatch and, for good measure, weighed it down with an anchor. Shiers set off to capture the mate Tait.

---

8   The expression 'under the rose' referred to something to be kept secret, not discussed with outsiders. In that era, pubs were often decorated with carved roses on the ceiling, to indicate that anything said there should not be repeated outside those walls. The tradition goes back at least as far as Roman times, where banquet rooms had roses painted on the ceilings. The Latin term *sub rosa*, means 'in secret'.

He returned to the deck with Tait under guard, where they joined Jimmy, James Leslie, and Leslie's prisoner, the fourth soldier. At this point Jimmy opened the hatch again to allow the five convicts down below to rejoin their triumphant mates on deck. He then ordered Tait and the soldier to go down to join the other soldier, and the convicts resealed the hatch. So two soldiers and Tait were now sealed below decks. However, that created a new problem. The ship's gun store was also below decks, and the soldiers could move around down there without being detected by those up on deck. If the soldiers had thought and acted quickly enough, they might have rearmed themselves. The convicts crept aft and gingerly went below decks to the gun store. This had to be done with great stealth, but luck was with them. They removed all the muskets and ball cartridges without interference, and brought them up on deck. They now had a near monopoly on arms aboard the *Frederick*, and a large measure of control of the ship.

That left Captain Taw, David Hoy and the steward Nichols still aboard the *Frederick* and not captured by the convicts. Taw and Hoy were in the captain's cabin, drinking rum. There seems to be universal agreement that Taw was staggering drunk, a not unusual state of affairs. There is some dispute over the whereabouts and actions of the steward Nichols. The version that follows is from David Hoy. It largely matches Jimmy Porter's Norfolk Island account.

According to Hoy, two convicts, one of whom was William Shiers, burst into the captain's cabin. Shiers put a pistol to Hoy's head and said: 'We have the vessel, and if you don't give yourself up we will blow your brains out.' Hoy tried to wrestle the pistol away from Shiers, while Taw did his drunken best to wrestle with the other convict, who was armed with the tomahawk and possibly a musket.

Hoy kept calling out to the soldiers for help, but his shouts understandably went unanswered. According to Jimmy, the convicts on deck then opened the skylight and looked down into Taw's cabin. There they saw Shiers wrestling with Hoy, and a general melee. Finally Shiers broke away from Hoy, while the other convict escaped Taw's drunken clutches, and the two convicts raced up the cabin stairs towards the deck. They did this, in Jimmy's words: 'Before we could render him [Shiers] any assistance.' In Hoy's version, the steward Nichols was standing at the foot of the stairs but was either unable or unwilling to do anything to block the convicts' passage, and the two convicts reached the deck unscathed.

Hoy, who knew the ship inside out, now tried to open up a passage through the bulkhead between Captain Taw's cabin and the soldiers' quarters next door. He managed to get a glimpse into the soldiers' living space but saw neither soldiers nor guns there, so there was no point continuing. Meanwhile, the convicts were shouting from the deck above: 'Come up and save your lives.' They called to Hoy and Taw by name, telling them if they did not give themselves up they would be shot.

Hoy now tried another ploy. He called out to the convicts that if they would lay down their arms and go back to their duties, the whole affair would be forgotten and there would be no repercussions. This didn't go down well with the convicts, who shouted back that they had their freedom, and they would rather die than give it up.

It is not uncommon for a drunk to peel off his coat and offer to fight every man in the bar, and Taw proceeded to do more or less that. He asked Hoy where Hoy's pistols were. Hoy replied that they were in his sea chest. Taw announced that he had only a musket, but that they must sell their lives dearly. Hoy went to open his sea chest to find his pistols, when one of the convicts fired through the open skylight, sending a musket ball through the chest, near the lock. Hoy stepped back, whereupon a second musket shot went through the chest about 8 inches (20 centimetres) from the first.

Hoy nevertheless managed to open his sea chest and grab his pistols. He shouted that he intended to shoot the first man he saw through the skylight. The convicts shouted back that if those below came up on deck and surrendered, no harm would come to them. This rather fruitless back-and-forth shouting match is said to have continued for about an hour and a half. Then the convicts began to lose patience. Some wanted to shoot Hoy and Taw there and then. Others advised caution; they did not want blood on their hands. Finally, one called out: 'Bring along the pitch pot [hot tar pot] and let us empty it down on them.' At this point Taw and Hoy conferred, and agreed that it would be 'a wilful waste of life' if they held out any longer. They, together with the steward Nichols, agreed to surrender. The *Frederick* was now totally in convict hands.

That still left the fishing party on the loose, and possibly armed. According to Jimmy, the prearranged signal for the whaleboat to return was a musket shot fired from the deck of the *Frederick*. There had, of course, already been two musket shots fired by the convicts at Hoy's sea chest, so the signal had been well and truly given. Nevertheless, the convicts decided to fire off a third musket shot, which produced the required result. The whaleboat came alongside.[9]

The fishing party were told that the brig had been seized. They were ordered to tie the whaleboat securely to the *Frederick* and to lower the ship's dinghy (known as the 'jolly boat'), usually suspended from the stern. The fishing party did as they were told, while an armed convict stood guard to prevent them from coming aboard the brig. Jimmy Porter, John Barker and William Shiers then escorted Taw and Hoy back to their cabin,[10] where the two men collected their clothing. They had already been told they would be put ashore while the brig sailed away.

Not all was sweetness and light. As Jimmy records in his journal: 'We allowed them to take anything they wanted—they wanted a pistol and some ammunition from us to protect them from the blacks (as they wished to make us believe), but we

---

9 It is not clear why the shot was required, as there were no collaborators aboard the whaleboat.

10 In a later account, Hoy stated under oath that only Barker and Shiers had accompanied him and Captain Taw down below, and that Jimmy Porter had not been present. The above account comes from Jimmy's Norfolk Island journal, the main intention of which was to glorify Jimmy's role in these proceedings.

begged to be excused!!!' Having collected their clothing, Taw and Hoy climbed back on deck under the watchful eyes of the armed and triumphant convicts. At this point, Barker ordered Hoy to hand over his watch. According to Jimmy, Taw was also ordered to hand over *his* watch. Hoy also had a small pocket compass, which would come in handy if he and the other non-convicts tried to make their way across country to civilisation. Shiers, out of earshot of Barker, ordered Hoy to hang onto it. Hoy had complained earlier of feeling ill, so Shiers gave Hoy a bottle of spirits wrapped in a shirt, and told him to keep it out of sight. Hoy did as he was told.

Tait and the two soldiers were now ordered up from the forecastle, where they had remained, and joined Hoy and Taw on deck. All non-conspirators—Captain Taw and David Hoy, the mate Tait, the steward Nichols, the free man McFarlane, and the four soldiers—were ordered into the jolly boat, and the convicts instructed them to 'pull for the shore'. Meanwhile, six armed convicts untied the whaleboat, and two convicts rowed it towards the shore, following in the wake of the jolly boat, while the other four stood guard. When the jolly boat reached the beach, the convicts in the whaleboat told the occupants to go ashore. They then ordered the men on shore to push the empty jolly boat back into deeper water— in Jimmy's words, 'to prevent them from rushing upon our boat'. The convicts took the jolly boat in tow, and headed back to the brig.

Ten convicts, well armed, now had complete charge of the *Frederick* and its two small boats. All nine non-conspirators had been put ashore with ample clothing but no arms and no supplies. And not a drop of blood had been spilt.

———————

The convicts treated themselves to a good dinner. The settlement's remaining provisions were on board, enough to last nineteen men for three months, so there was plenty to go around. The next morning they brought all the provisions up on deck and divided them equally, the same share for the nine men ashore as for the ten men aboard the *Frederick*. David Hoy explained what followed:

> Saw a boat the next morning come from the brig to the shore; went towards the boat but was told not to come near, or they would not land what they had got for us; they landed some provisions, and different articles belonging to the military, such as knapsacks, coats, &c; this was between 6 and 7 in the morning. The boat returned a second time with some flannels, some dressing and a pair of shoes. Shiers was in the boat the second time; I had been asking all along for the boat, but was told we could not have one till the brig went over the bar, when they would send one, with some more provisions, to the pilot's house; we went to the pilot's house the same day the boat came; but no boat was sent to us; nor did we receive anything more from the ship.

The convicts had handed over 181 pounds (82 kilograms) of meat, 261 pounds (118 kilograms) of biscuits, and 61 pounds

(28 kilograms) of flour; there had been plenty of potatoes and cabbages growing at the pilot's house near the entrance to the harbour, and these were shared out too, along with a live goat, an iron pot, two or three tin pannikins, and an axe. The convicts awarded themselves the same rations, without the goat. There were ten mouths to feed ashore (nine men and a goat), and eleven to feed on the *Frederick*—ten convicts and the ship's cat.

If we are to believe Jimmy, there was then an emotional farewell worthy of the most sentimental Victorian melodrama. Jimmy reports Hoy as declaring: 'I thank you for your manly conduct throughout, and particularly for your kindness to me on account of my illness. I know you have but little provisions to cross the wide ocean, and likewise a vessel that is not Seaworthy for such a voyage—and may God preserve you in your perilous undertaking.' Jimmy adds his own bit of equally improbable melodrama:

> We thanked him and pulled off our hats amid the loud cheers of all on shore wishing us a Pleasant Voyage. I cannot express my feelings at that moment—my heart expanded within me and I believe it was the happiest moment of my life. We observed Mr Hoy wiping his eyes. We felt for him and that was all we could do in our situation.

Sounds like pure soap opera.

———

Hoy could not recall the exact date when the *Frederick* sailed out of Macquarie Harbour, but he was inclined to think it must have been either 15 or 16 January 1834, four or five days after the initial launch of the brig. Jimmy puts the date at 14 January, which fits the facts better. Whatever the date, it was certainly an emotional moment for Hoy (if perhaps not for the reasons Jimmy gives). The *Frederick* had been his pride and joy, though he rightly worried that it was not seaworthy, and it was certainly not ready for any long sea voyage. It showed signs of leaking, for instance. He watched wistfully as the *Frederick* cleared the bar safely and turned southwest, away from Macquarie Harbour and towards the fierce winds of the Antarctic Ocean. He never saw the ship again.

Part 4

CHILE

Edward Willmann's 1840 print shows the thriving and busy Valparaiso harbour as it must have looked when Royal Navy ships were based there. At the time, it was the Royal Navy's South America Station. (Alamy)

The road between Valparaiso and Santiago, depicted by the French naturalist Claude ('Claudio') Gay. The etching is almost certainly from the years 1834–43, when Gay lived in Santiago. Jimmy Porter's marriage to Narcissa Martel took place around 1820, and her parents gave the young couple a farm situated along this road. Travelling along the road must have been quite an adventure. (iStock)

The Iglesia de la Matriz del Salvador is in the port district of Valparaiso. It was much frequented in the eighteenth and nineteenth centuries by the wealthy and fashionable families of Valparaiso, so it is a fair guess that Jimmy and Narcissa were married there. In 1822 it was flattened in an earthquake and had to be rebuilt.

An 1830 engraving by Edward Duncan from a painting by W.J. Huggins, Marine Painter to His Majesty, shows Hobart harbour in the mid-1820s, a few years after Jimmy first arrived. At that time, Hobart was still not much bigger than a village, but the multi-story buildings in the distance are evidence of an ambitious building program. (NLA)

This undated drawing or painting is an important record of the improvements to the penal colony at Sarah Island. Based on the elaborate fencing and building work, it must have been created well after the arrival of Captain James Butler as commandant in April 1825. (Tasmanian Archives, NS1013-1-1866)

Both Charles Constantini and Thomas Lempriere were prolific recorders of Sarah Island life, and this undated watercolour is likely by one of them. Constantini was a convict sentenced to transportation for forgery; Lempriere was not a convict but the commissariat officer, in charge of all Macquarie Harbour stores including food, clothing and medical supplies. (NLA)

RELICS OF CONVICT DISCIPLINE.   BEATTIE-HOBART.

A gruesome collection of manacles, leg-irons, handcuffs, a ball and chain and firearms—some of the equipment used for convict 'discipline'. The whip or cat-o'-nine-tails in the picture is an altogether less cruel device than the Sarah Island whip, or 'thief's cat', which was designed to cut and injure, not just to inflict pain. (NLA)

An 1830 drawing showing Philips Island cultivation. The scene it depicts is more romantic than accurate. Philips Island, one of three work sites for convict gangs, was a few kilometres north of Sarah Island, inside Macquarie Harbour. There were endless attempts to grow potatoes and wheat on the island, but the wheat crop regularly failed. (NLA)

An old black and white photograph of the site of the original docks on Sarah Island, where the *Frederick* was likely built. (Tasmanian Archives, AB713-1-3948)

Lempriere's 1831 sketch shows a ship entering Macquarie Harbour via Hell's Gates, as seen from the pilot's station. The small islands partially blocking the narrow channel added to the already considerable difficulties of navigating the heads. The nine men in the bottom left corner of the drawing appear to be launching a large rowboat, presumably the pilot boat. (Tasmanian Archives, SD_ILS 653853)

A 1952 etching by Lieutenant Commander Geoffrey Ingleton, *The Brig FREDERICK departs from Sarah's Island, Macquarie Harbour, VDL*. Ingleton's drawing meticulously and accurately depicts the *Frederick*'s appearance and rigging. However, it is unlikely that the *Frederick* would have been under full sail approaching the narrow and tricky harbour exit at Hell's Gates. (NLA)

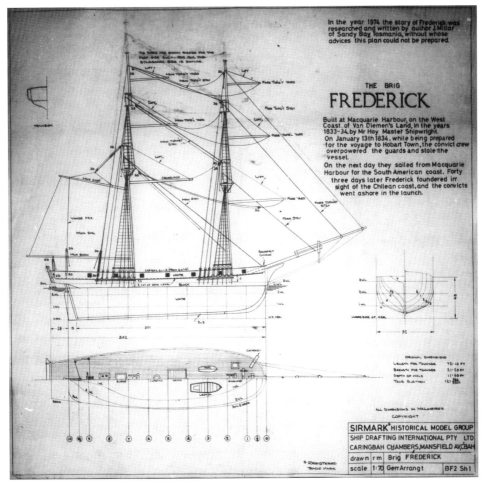

In the year 1974 the story of Frederick was researched and written by author J.Millar of Sandy Bay Tasmania, without whose advices this plan could not be prepared.

THE BRIG
FREDERICK

Built at Macquarie Harbour, on the West Coast of Van Diemen's Land, in the years 1833-34, by Mr Hoy Master Shipwright.
On January 13th 1834, while being prepared for the voyage to Hobart Town, the convict crew overpowered the guards and stole the vessel.
On the next day they sailed from Macquarie Harbour for the South American coast. Forty three days later Frederick foundered in sight of the Chilean coast, and the convicts went ashore in the launch.

SIRMARK HISTORICAL MODEL GROUP
SHIP DRAFTING INTERNATIONAL PTY LTD
CARINGBAH CHAMBERS, MANSFIELD AV.CBAH

| drawn | r m | Brig FREDERICK | |
| scale | 1:70 | Genl Arrangt | BF2 Sh1 |

This plan of the *Frederick* was for ship modellers, so it illustrates what the ship looked like from the outside but not below decks. There were probably two more deck levels below the open main deck. The captain's cabin was usually at the stern (rear) of the ship, on the middle deck (the upper of the two levels), while the forecastle (fo'c'sle) will have been at the bow end, on the same deck as the captain's cabin. The soldiers' quarters were next to the captain's cabin. The lower level was the hold, used for carrying cargo and probably housing the pumps.

The plan shows a large hatch on the open top deck between the masts, and this will have been the main access to the middle deck via a steep flight of stairs. It also shows a smaller hatch (marked 'access') on the top deck just to the rear of the main mast. This must have been the hatch to the captain's cabin. There will have been a large hatch on the middle deck, again probably between the masts and directly below the large hatch on the open deck, allowing access to the hold.
(Tasmanian Archives, PH30/1/2879)

An engraving of a Valdivia street scene in the spring of 1835 gives a good idea of the life and atmosphere of a provincial Chilean town at the time Jimmy arrived there. The church on the left suggests that the street was fairly central to the town, yet the dirt road probably became a mudbath after rain and most buildings have been constructed of wood. (Alamy)

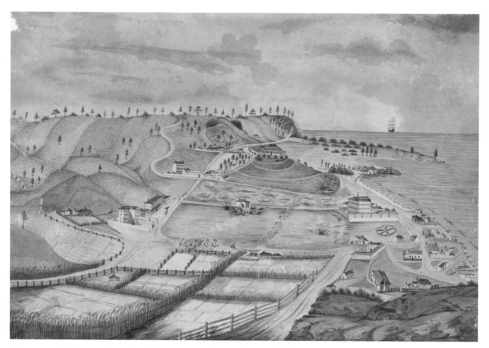

Thomas Seller painted this watercolour of Norfolk Island in 1839, around the time Jimmy was 'transported' there. Seller was an engineer and free man who held the position of foreman of works on the island. The painting is an optimistic version of what was likely a much less orderly and productive scene. (NLA)

Chapter 8

VOYAGE

The press had a field day. The 7 February 1834 issue of the *Hobart Town Courier* set the tone of gleeful handwringing. In those days newspapers carried classified advertisements on their front page and tucked the news away inside.[1] On page two of the *Courier*, after a brief gallop through the bushfire news, the newspaper swung its keen eye in the direction of Sarah Island and the latest outrage. 'We have the pain this week to announce another of those daring acts of piracy which from time to time have disgraced the annals of these colonies,' it lamented. There followed a lip-smacking account of the treacherous ingenuity of the convicts in overwhelming the legal masters of the *Frederick*. The *Courier* averred that it was a severe lesson for the authorities:

This unfortunate occurrence, which has, it is needless to disguise it, been occasioned by a repetition of the same negligence which was so instrumental in producing the

---

1 *The Times* of London kept up this quaint practice until 3 May 1966.

loss of the *Cyprus*, will, we trust, be a caution on all future occasions, especially to the military.

The *Courier* even went so far as to suggest that Captain Taw and David Hoy might have tried a bit harder. 'We must say,' the newspaper concluded in convoluted prose, 'that with such numbers and with such a guard and furnished with arms too, we regret that any appearance of supineness was evinced, and that a more determined resistance was not made even after the surprise that appears to have been used, which if it had we cannot help thinking that the piracy would have been prevented'.

The *Courier* spoke for the whole colony in pointing out that the authorities had not exactly covered themselves in glory. Everybody was laughing at them, and no government likes that.

———

The *Courier* did not go into detail about how the nine men left behind at Macquarie Harbour had survived. It merely reported: 'Capt. Taw, Mr Hoy, and the others who were sent on shore afterwards, made the best of their way to Circular Head, from whence Capt. Taw proceeded to Launceston, and by the mail [mail boat] to Hobart town on Tuesday morning.'

Circular Head is on the northwest corner of Tasmania, and is a good solid walk from Macquarie Harbour. The distance is about 220 kilometres through dense forest. It would be possible to walk via the coast, but this would add distance and involve an awkward crossing of the Arthur River. The overland distance from Circular Head to Launceston is about another

230 kilometres, so that would have been an even longer walk. There is every possibility that Captain Taw made his way by sea from Circular Head, which was a small port, to Launceston, a river port. That would certainly have been quicker than walking, or even travelling on horseback.

Whatever the route and mode of transport, the nine men seem to have overcome their problems quickly. Taw arrived in Hobart on 4 February, three weeks after he and his companions had been unceremoniously dumped on the mainland shore of Macquarie Harbour without so much as a rowboat. Thus did the news of the capture of the brig travel fast, via Captain Taw.

Having cleared the treacherous bar at the entrance to Macquarie Harbour, the convicts aboard the *Frederick* had a simple and urgent problem. The brig's non-arrival would be noticed in Hobart, so the authorities would be bound to send someone to find out what was going on. Ships travelling between Hobart and the settlement tended to pass through Bass Strait along the north coast of Van Diemen's Land, where the weather was not quite as bad as on the west coast. If the convicts wanted literally to steer clear of authority, their best bet was to chance the rough seas and violent winds to the west and south of the colony.

Nor would government ships be their only problem. The ten convicts knew that as soon as their escape was known, the authorities would issue a description of the missing brig. The description the *Courier* later published read:

The brig may be known at sea by its billet head, flush deck, quarter pieces,[2] painted ports, seven on each side—main topsail half worn, considerably too small for the size of the ship—no square main sail, though the pirates may probably bend a cutter's square sail for a main course. With the exception of the foresail, which is new, all the other sails are half worn.

Every vessel the convicts came across would be a potential threat, capable of identifying them and reporting their whereabouts and course to the authorities.

Being spotted was not their only concern. Their ship was already leaking, and bad weather would only make things worse. But they had little choice. They set a course east-southeast from their position outside the entrance to Macquarie Harbour. This would take them down the coast and around the wild southern tip of Van Diemen's Land. They manned the pumps.

There are only two existing accounts of the voyage of the *Frederick*, and Jimmy Porter wrote both of them. As mentioned, the two accounts disagree on detail, and sometimes contradict one another, depending on Jimmy's target audience. However, they are the only accounts available. Where the two accounts clash, I have simply settled on what I judged to be the most plausible version.

━━━ ━━━

---

2   Usually a pair of decorated balconies towards the rear of the ship.

The convicts aboard the *Frederick* were not well equipped for a long sea voyage. They had no charts, for instance. The most sophisticated piece of navigation equipment they had was a quadrant, a large, old and clumsy version of the sextant still used by sea navigators today. Like a sextant, the quadrant could measure the angle between the horizon and the sun, and could also determine when the sun was at its highest point above the horizon. When the sun is at its highest, the local time is noon.

The angle between the sun and the horizon at noon would determine latitude, while the difference between the time at a datum (usually the Greenwich meridian or 0°) and noon aboard the ship would allow the navigator to determine the ship's longitude. In skilful hands, a quadrant and a good clock used together could pinpoint a ship's position fairly accurately.

Measuring the time difference, however, would need a very accurate clock, usually called a chronometer. This was the significance of the convicts' seizure of David Hoy's and Captain Taw's watches. Today the word 'watch' usually refers to a small timepiece worn on the wrist. Watch mechanisms today are very often 'quartz', which means the watch is battery driven and keeps accurate time for months at a stretch. But in 1834 a 'watch' was usually what we would now call a 'fob watch', an institution that has largely disappeared from 21st-century lives.

A fob watch was four or five times the size of a modern wristwatch, and much heavier. It usually hung from the end of a chain, and was tucked into the fob pocket of the wearer's waistcoat. The mechanism was driven by a wind-up spring, which meant it had to be wound daily or it would stop. In general, spring mechanism watches were not accurate enough for navigation, as they gained or lost several minutes a day. However, some of the better fob watches were accurate enough to be used as chronometers,[3] and that probably applied to the watches carried by Hoy and Taw.

Without a chart, the information supplied by the quadrant was of limited value anyway. Suppose the navigator, John Barker (who was also acting as captain),[4] having taken his quadrant readings and consulted his various navigation tables, had been able to pinpoint the ship's position as 17°20' south, 149°35' west. Without a chart, that would not tell him whether the island off the starboard bow was Tahiti (French and good) or Pitcairn Island (full of British mutiny-on-the-*Bounty* descendants and bad). Barker will have known that the coast of Chile ran from a northern border with Peru at about 18° south to Cape Horn at about 55° south, and that cities like Valparaiso were in the middle at about 33° south. So if the *Frederick* could keep

---

3   I have a fob watch from the nineteenth century, a family heirloom, marked inside: *Sir John Bennett, 65 Cheapside, London, Maker to the Royal Observatory*. Insofar as the Royal Observatory was the custodian of the Greenwich meridian, it is a safe bet that this watch kept good enough time to be used for navigation. In his advertising, Bennett often referred to a fob watch made by him as a 'chronometer'.

4   Readers may wonder why John Barker was chosen as captain when he had no sailing experience and there were four experienced sailors in the crew. The answer seems to be that John Barker carried a natural authority and had obvious leadership skills. Such was his formidable personality that even the Sarah Island guards called him 'Mr Barker' instead of plain 'Barker'.

sailing across the Pacific Ocean in an easterly direction, and stay between 18° and 55° south, the voyage would end in Chile.

Barker did most of his navigation by what is known as 'dead reckoning'. This simply consists of saying that the boat is *here* and travelling in a certain direction at a certain speed and therefore must have sailed from *here* to *there* after a certain time. Dead reckoning cannot take ocean currents into account, and is not much better than informed guesswork. Most sailors would agree that any position arrived at by dead reckoning will be not too far out after one day, fairly unreliable after a few days, and totally useless after a week. Barker sailed by dead reckoning for weeks on end.

The other big consideration was the wind and the weather. This book is a historical narrative, not a textbook on meteorology, and anybody with even a rudimentary knowledge of that subject will flinch at the generalisations that follow. Nevertheless, a few broad principles will not go amiss.

As a huge generalisation, because of the earth's rotation and other factors, the world's surface air near the equator tends to flow from east to west; surface air in the mid-latitudes tends to flow west to east; and surface air near the poles tends to flow from east to west again.[5] The surface winds blow accordingly. There are massive local variations, and localised weather systems that send winds in different directions, but the general principle holds good.

---

5   The upper air is a different story. It tends to flow from west to east everywhere, which is why your flight from London to New York regularly takes an hour longer than the flight from New York to London.

As a further generalisation, weather systems begin at an imaginary line in the ocean where warm equatorial waters meet cold polar waters. The line shifts with the seasons: in the southern hemisphere it moves south in the summer and north in the winter. A kink in the line, given a shove from behind by the earth's rotation, will create a depression. From modest low-pressure areas to legendary, howling storms, the bulk of the world's weather systems start at this imaginary line. As the *Frederick*'s journey began in the southern summer month of January, the line will have shifted to somewhere around 55° south.

So the convicts aboard the *Frederick* faced some invidious choices. If they took the *Frederick* north—say, between the equator and 25° south—they would be sailing mostly into wind, and running the risk of fighting end-of-season tropical storms. As well, they could find themselves too far north and miss Chile altogether, landing in less-friendly Peru instead. If they stayed in the middle latitudes—between 25° and 55° south, say— then they would have following winds and milder weather. However, they would not be alone: most other ships would be doing the same, so their chances of being spotted and either attacked or reported would be much greater. Finally, they could opt for a much shorter southerly route, between 55° south and the South Pole. In this case they would be sailing into the wind, in the notoriously wild Antarctic Ocean, with the risk of icebergs and other hazards in their path.

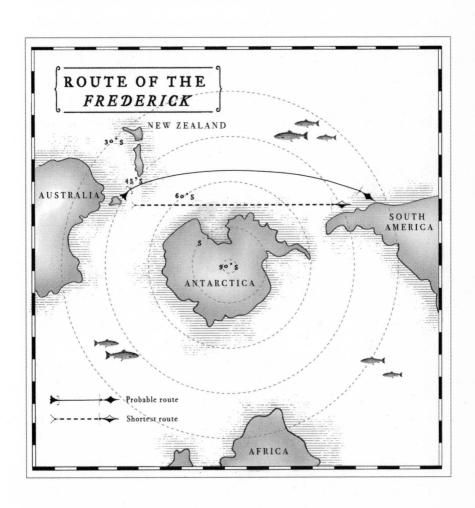

ROUTE OF THE
FREDERICK

NEW ZEALAND

30° S

45° S

AUSTRALIA

60° S

S

90° S

ANTARCTICA

SOUTH
AMERICA

AFRICA

Probable route
Shortest route

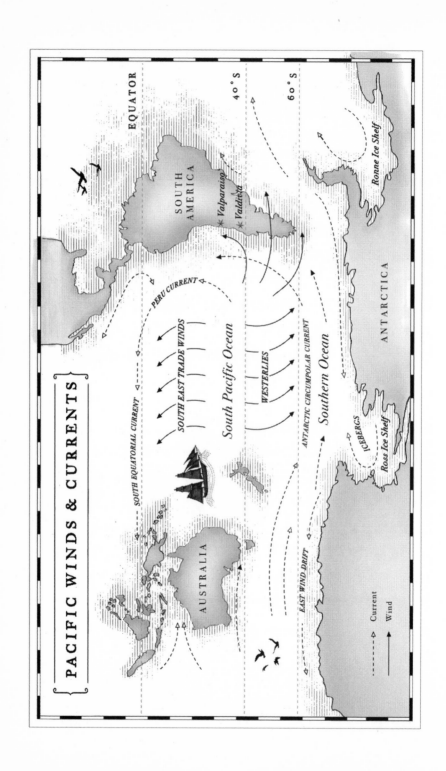

PACIFIC WINDS & CURRENTS

EQUATOR

40° S

60° S

SOUTH AMERICA

*Valparaiso
*Valdivia

Ronne Ice Shelf

ANTARCTICA

PERU CURRENT

SOUTH EAST TRADE WINDS

South Pacific Ocean

WESTERLIES

ANTARCTIC CIRCUMPOLAR CURRENT

Southern Ocean

SOUTH EQUATORIAL CURRENT

ICEBERGS

Ross Ice Shelf

AUSTRALIA

EAST WIND DRIFT

- - - - - Current
———— Wind

The journey started at Macquarie Harbour, which is about 42° south. John Barker first set course to take the *Frederick* around the southern tip of Tasmania, which is a bit beyond 43° south. So the ship and its convict crew began by committing themselves to the southern half of the mid-latitudes. This zone is well known to sailors, to the point of being notorious: not for nothing are the winds referred to as the Roaring Forties.

The voyage had barely got underway when the wind sprang up from the northwest. The *Frederick* was now making 12 knots, a very decent speed, with only two sails hoisted, a main topsail and a foresail. The tailwind was so strong that it needed two men to handle the helm. Hoy's warning about leaks proved to be only too true. In Jimmy's words: 'We got the pumps to work and they were kept going all the voyage—we dare not neglect them two hours at a time.'[6] There were four experienced seamen on board: Jimmy, Charles Lyon, John Jones and John Fair. They divided themselves into two watches, making sure there were two seamen who knew what they were doing on each watch.

The strong winds continued and heavily reduced the effectiveness of the makeshift crew. Five of the ten suffered badly from seasickness, most notably the 'captain', John Barker. The rough seas also sent William Shiers, Benjamin Russen, William Cheshire and James Leslie down below. Happily, none of the

---

6 Two men were required to work each pump, which they did by either winding a flywheel handle or using a rocker handle. It was hard manual labour.

experienced sailors was forced to take to his bunk, and they and John Dady bore the brunt of the work until the invalids found their sea legs. Throughout this time the crew faced one of those insoluble dilemmas: they needed to go fast to be sure of staying ahead of any pursuers, but the more they piled on sail, the more the *Frederick* leaked, and the more water the exhausted crew had to pump.

———

John Barker recovered from his seasickness, and at noon on 16 January, two days after the journey began, he was able to take a quadrant reading, which placed the *Frederick* below the southern tip of Van Diemen's Land. Barker now altered course from east-southeast to southeast, pushing the *Frederick* further south, further into the Roaring Forties. The new course was necessary to take the brig south of the South Island of New Zealand, while still staying clear of the main shipping lanes. The southernmost point in New Zealand is Stewart Island, which is about 47° south.[7] So the *Frederick*'s push into cold and stormy southern waters continued with renewed vigour.

Barker began to worry that the brig was sailing too far south. He ordered a new course a little more to the east. This brought the brig, as sailors say, 'nearer the wind'—the friendly following wind became more of a side wind, making the brig harder to handle. If Jimmy is to be believed, at one point Charles Lyon

---

7   The Campbell Islands, at roughly 52° south and claimed for New Zealand, were discovered in 1810 and only frequented by sealers and whalers.

at the helm lost his nerve and swung the ship back onto its old course, to take advantage of the easier sailing with a following wind. This was not noticed until the next day, when Barker's quadrant reading showed the ship was 'scores of miles' out of position. There must have been some kind of informal trial among the convicts when this treachery was discovered. In Jimmy's words: 'When the rascals were taxed with this gross neglect of duty they told the truth, and we were going to give Lyon a short passage over the side—but all ended in peace and it was looked over with a caution not to do the like again at his peril or he should certainly DIE.'

———

The convicts had given away half their provisions, and the food they kept was hardly going to last them the whole distance to Chile. They rationed the little they had, caught fish when they could, and collected rainwater.

Then Barker fell ill again. At one point he stayed below decks for nine days; no quadrant readings were taken during this time, which meant the ship was sailing on blind faith and the deadest of dead reckoning. There was a scare when the convicts spotted vast quantities of seaweed in the ocean. Seaweed needs warm water to flourish. Was the *Frederick* too far north? The men begged Barker to come up on deck and take a look. Barker took a cursory look at the seaweed, and the position of the sun, and announced: 'Do not be in the least dubious as to my knowledge or capability of performing what I have taken in hand, for I can take you safe to South America, even although

I had no quadrant on board, for I could do it by keeping a dead reckoning, it being a straight course.' The men took him at his word, having no choice in the matter.

———

On 31 January, seventeen days into the journey, Barker was well enough to take another quadrant reading. Miraculously, the brig was not too far out of position. However, in the light of the new reading, Barker was able to alter course to northeast, still with favourable winds. The more northerly course eased the *Frederick* away from the worst of the southern weather. Barker informed his fellow convicts that he intended to make landfall in Chile somewhere between the ports of Valparaiso and Valdivia. This generous target gives some measure of the vagueness of Barker's navigation: Valdivia, at 39° of latitude, is more than 750 kilometres south of Valparaiso at 33°.

It is worth pointing out here that the port of Valparaiso was then a major British naval base, known as the South America Station. (Its name later changed to the Pacific Station.) It was headquarters to the Royal Navy's Pacific fleet, a status it had enjoyed since 1826. At the time of the *Frederick*'s voyage, the nominal commander-in-chief was Rear-Admiral Sir Michael Seymour. He had died *en route* to the station, and was not replaced until 16 September 1834, when Vice-Admiral Graham Hammond took command. Although the men on the *Frederick* could not have known it, the fact that there was no settled British commander in Valparaiso would be likely to work in their favour.

However, none of these comings and goings would have been of much interest to the ten convicts as they battled wind, weather and a leaky boat, not to mention starvation rations. All they knew was that if Barker made their landfall too close to Valparaiso, they could expect trouble. So south it had to be.

On 27 February 1834, six weeks and one day[8] after they set off from Macquarie Harbour, the convicts sighted land. The high mountains they could see on the horizon had to be Chile. They'd made it.

By any standard, this was an incredible feat. After the famous mutiny on the *Bounty* in 1789, Lieutenant William Bligh was rightly celebrated for sailing the *Bounty*'s launch some 4000 miles from mid-Pacific to Timor, thereby saving his own life and the lives of eighteen loyal members of his crew. Like the convicts, Bligh had no charts. He also had a quadrant, but no chronometer.

In terms of distance covered, even Bligh's voyage pales before the achievement of the *Frederick*. The exact distance Bligh sailed was 6701 kilometres (4164 miles). The straight-line distance from Macquarie Harbour to the coast of Chile is

---

8 Readers of a mathematical bent may wonder why the length of the journey is not six weeks and two days, given that the *Frederick* left Macquarie Harbour on 14 January. However, the departure date is far from certain, and the ship had to cross the International Date Line, which meant the doubling up of a day in the lives of the crew. The figure of six weeks and one day is from Jimmy Porter's Norfolk Island journal.

10,837 kilometres (6734 miles), but in fact the convicts had sailed much further because the shortest great circle route[9] was not available to them. They had to deviate to the south to sail around New Zealand, and then deviate well north of the shortest route to make best use of the prevailing wind and to avoid the horrendous Antarctic Ocean weather. They must have sailed roughly twice as far as Bligh, with short rations and equally limited navigation equipment, without so much as a chart to tell them where they were. It was a staggering example of seamanship, courage, skill and daring.

Jimmy is forthcoming about the difficulties they faced. They reached land just in time: 'The brig was getting the best of us in the leakage.' They became so worried about the leaks that they used what little strength they had left to get their 7-ton longboat out on deck 'in case we should have to quit the Brig'.

They could feel well pleased with themselves. They had crossed more than 10,000 kilometres of stormy ocean on starvation rations in a leaky, unfamiliar and untried ship. Here they were, thousands of miles from their oppressors, still alive, and free.

A new and better life could begin the next day.

---

9   Because the earth is round, the shortest route between two points is seldom the obvious one drawn on a standard Mercator's Projection map. If you put a piece of string on a globe with the string running between the starting point and the end point of a journey, and pull the string tight, the string's path is the 'great circle route' between the two points.

Chapter 9

VALDIVIA

Now that land was in sight, the convicts had a new problem. On landing in Chile, what story could they tell to explain who they were and how they got there? In 1834, if ten ragged and haggard seamen simply breezed into Valparaiso, or Valdivia, or any other Chilean port, without a convincing explanation, they could reasonably expect to be taken for pirates, and promptly hanged or shot. The men decided that claiming to be shipwrecked sailors might get them some sympathy, and it would also explain why they had no papers, no money, no possessions, no cargo, no obvious mission, and no one expecting them. They rehearsed their stories in preparation for the inevitable questioning. William Cheshire was less diligent than the others, leading Jimmy to wonder if he could be relied on to stick to the story.

It is hard to avoid the feeling that the *Frederick* itself deserved a better fate than that finally handed out to it by the convicts. Though land was perhaps as much as 60 or 70 kilometres away, they decided to abandon the leaking and sinking brig and take to the longboat. Jimmy describes the *Frederick*'s sorry end:

> We got the long boat out with great difficulty and put what little things we had into her. As for provisions we had not more than 2 pounds [a bit less than 1.1 kilogram] of bread and meat—we dropped the long boat astern and sloop rigged her.[10] We had neglected pumping the vessel ever since we sighted land, being employed at other things. We found the sooner we got out of her the better, and it was not until dark that night we could leave her, being fairly knocked up with over-exertion and little to eat. However, we took our leave of her, hove her to as she was approaching shore which we calculated about 40 miles off—and I never left my parents with more regret nor was my feelings harrowed up to such a pitch as when I took a last farewell of the smart little *Frederick*. The brig stood to seaward, and in the state she was in, water-logged and so much dead weight for ballast—she soon went down.

So the *Frederick* sank, taking with her the ship's papers and everything else, to the bottom of the Pacific Ocean.

———

The convicts spent their first Chilean night in the longboat, under sail and heading for shore. It is impossible to say with

---

10 This means that they rigged the whale boat with a single mast which carried a mainsail and a foresail.

any confidence where they made landfall. Jimmy says they rowed into a 'large bay', where they sheltered and gathered shellfish.

Animal lovers will be pleased to hear that all eleven souls had survived the journey from Macquarie Harbour to Chile— ten convicts and the ship's cat. No sooner had they landed than the cat showed that independence of spirit for which cats are rightly famous and skedaddled into the bush. It spent the night there, slinking back to the camp the next morning, then promptly scarpered again, this time for good. Jimmy's Norfolk Island journal informs us that if only they had followed the cat they would have come to the mouth of the 'Rio Beuon'[11] and a large Indian settlement, which would have 'saved us a deal of trouble'.

The convicts killed a seal and left a few bits of it for the cat. Then they returned to the longboat to continue their search for friendly faces.

Jimmy reports that they followed the Chilean coast for some six days and nights. He doesn't tell us whether they were travelling north or south, so we can only guess at where they were and which way they were facing. The next landmark

---

11 If there is a River Beuon in Chile, then neither Google Earth nor *The Times Atlas of the World* has heard of it. However, a little to the south of Valdivia there is a Rio Bueno ('Good River'), which Wikipedia says is a promising place to fish. The river even gives its name to the town of Rio Bueno at the heart of Ranco Province in the southern Chilean region of Los Rios ('The Rivers'). Everything Jimmy tells us is consistent with the idea that their first landfall was near the mouth of the Rio Bueno. Captain Barker had just failed to hit his mark.

identified by Jimmy is 'Tweedale Point' ('Tweedle Point' in the Hobart journal), which he says 'projects a long way out to sea'. Jimmy tells us that the longboat took half an hour to round the point. When the convicts finally landed, some Chilean Indians told them that they were 'three leagues' (14 kilometres) from Valdivia. There is a large cape on the south side of the mouth of the Valdivia River, and the river mouth is also about the right distance from the port town of Valdivia, so it is at least a fair guess that the convicts landed on the cape at the mouth of the river, having sailed north from 'Rio Beuon'. According to Jimmy, the local Indians were also content with the encounter. 'We gave them a few trinkets, which pleased them much,' he reports. 'We took our departure, and the same afternoon we reached the port of Valdivia and landed safe, hungry enough.'

The convicts were initially well received when they landed near Valdivia. The local European population readily accepted that they were shipwrecked sailors and in need of help. Five of the convicts were taken to local houses, where they were treated hospitably. The remaining five stayed with the longboat. Four hours later, all ten reassembled at the boat, and spent the night there.

They now had a plan. They had been told that there was a shipyard in Valdivia in need of skilled workers. Five were experienced shipbuilders, and they immediately hired a canoe—for nine dollars, says Jimmy—and set off up the river to look for work. That left five staying behind with the longboat.

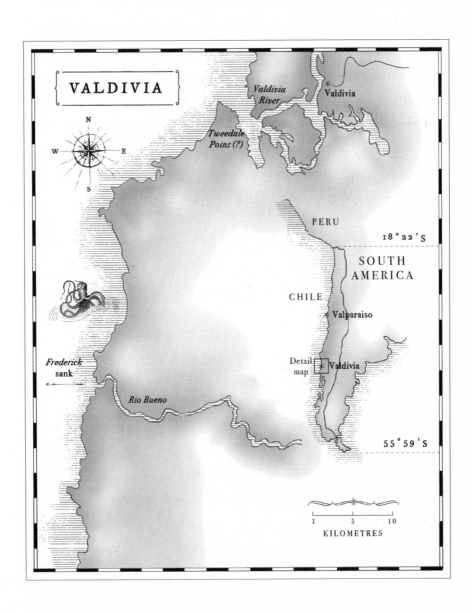

VALDIVIA

Valdivia River
Valdivia

Tweedale Point (?)

N
W E
S

PERU

18°22'S

SOUTH
AMERICA

CHILE

✳ Valparaiso

*Frederick
sank*

Detail
map   ✳ Valdivia

Rio Bueno

55°59'S

1   5   10

KILOMETRES

At this point in Jimmy's narrative the reader may feel that there is a dog in the night that has mysteriously failed to bark. What of Narcissa, Jimmy's wife? And what of their son, now a young teenager? They were last seen near Valparaiso about 700 kilometres north of Valdivia, but surely Jimmy's first thought after arriving in Chile would be to find out if they were still alive, where they were, and whether they had given up on him or would take him back in.

Jimmy continues:

> We bid them [i.e. the shipbuilding party] farewell for we never expected to see them again, as we intended to launch our boat the next day and get under way for Valparaiso where I knew if my wife, children and friends were alive I should remain during my life and return thanks to God that I did not founder on the rocks of despair.

That, dear reader, is the last you will hear from Jimmy of Narcissa and their teenage son.

Disaster struck the next day. The longboat had been trapped by the tide and could not be launched. Jimmy and his companions responded to this setback as anyone else might have done: they partied. 'We enjoyed ourselves very much with the Patriots, dancing and singing to the guitar,' Jimmy writes. They probably managed to slurp down their fair share of local hospitality along the way, because the following morning they slept in. That was their big mistake.

They were woken by a bunch of soldiers who had come to arrest them and take them upriver to Valdivia to be questioned by the governor.[12] They went with the soldiers in the longboat, and were promptly thrown into the same lock-up as their five fellow convicts, but kept separate from them. Jimmy used his limited Castilian Spanish to speak to one of the guards. Why had they been arrested? Apparently one of the other five had been drinking with a man called Cockney Tom, and had said rather too much about how they came to be in Chile. Jimmy already had it in for one of the five, William Cheshire, and he promptly blamed Cheshire for the debacle.

The convicts stayed in their Valdivian lock-up for three weeks before being brought before the governor. They were ushered into an elegant apartment with a large table in the centre. Governor Sanchez sat at one end of the table, while various officers of the Chilean military packed the room. A local smuggler called Captain Lawson acted as interpreter, and Jimmy assumed the role of spokesman for the convicts. He carefully went through the story the convicts had agreed upon. The governor was sceptical. Finally, Sanchez demanded: 'Call Thomas!' His call was answered by the appearance of Cockney Tom. The governor asked him: 'Is everything you told me privately true?' Cockney Tom answered with one word: 'Yes.' That was all Sanchez wanted to know. He declared: 'Sailors, you have come

---

12 Jimmy gives the governor's name as Sanchez in the Norfolk Island journal, and as Don Fernando Martelle in the Hobart journal. I have used 'Sanchez' in this narrative, largely because Fernando Martel (or Martell) is the correct name of Jimmy's father-in-law and this feels like a slip of the pen on Jimmy's part. Both names may have been inventions as there is no trace of either of these names in the records.

to this coast in a clandestine manner and though you put a good face on your story I have every reason to believe you are pirates. Unless you state the truth between now and tomorrow morning at 8 o'clock, I shall give orders for you all to be shot.'

For Jimmy it must have been a moment of déjà vu. It was, after all, his third death sentence . . . and counting.

———

What happened next is a matter for conjecture. Jimmy's two accounts tell widely different stories. Let's start with his Norfolk Island journal. There he says he called his fellow convicts together and persuaded them that only the truth could save them. They appeared before the governor the next morning. By now Jimmy was convinced that Cheshire would try to save his own skin by betraying the others. That made it all the more urgent to come out with the real story. So, in Jimmy's words: 'I told him the whole of our circumstances.' At this, Sanchez was mightily impressed and declared: 'I have no wish to keep you confined. If you will give me your word that you will not endeavour to make your escape, I will allow you to go about on Parole of Honour.'[13] The governor pointed out that there was plenty of work for them all, and in the meantime he would draw up a petition to the supreme governor in Santiago informing him that the men had thrown themselves on the protection of the Chilean authorities. Sanchez had no doubt that the response

---

13 That is, the governor agreed to take the convicts' word for it that they would not run away.

from Santiago would be favourable. Meanwhile, the convicts were free to go.

In the Hobart journal, Jimmy similarly states that they all went before the governor the next morning, whereupon Sanchez told them that 'he scarcely knew what to do about liberating us, as he was afraid some of us might endeavour to make our escape, by which those who were left behind would suffer'. In this version of events it is John Barker, not Jimmy, who makes the successful plea. Jimmy reports Barker as telling the governor:

> Sir, you need not be under any apprehension whatever of our making such an attempt; the privations we have all endured have been incredible, and our sufferings intense; therefore if, under the suspicion of our attempting such an act of ingratitude you should meditate delivering us up to the British government, I pray that you would rather do what would be a comparative act of charity, and give orders that we should all be shot dead in the palace square.

In this account, the speech from Barker reduced the governor to tears. After several minutes' silence—in which time Sanchez presumably recovered his composure—he announced: 'My poor men, do not think that I would take advantage over you; do not make an attempt to escape and I will be your friend; and, should a vessel come tomorrow to demand you, you will find that I shall be as good as my word.' In other words, you're free to go and will be safe here as long as you don't try to escape.

Jimmy continues the narrative:

We then thanked the Governor for his humanity, and took our leave, and went in search of lodgings, which we soon procured. The next day the whole of us attended in launching a vessel of four hundred tons burthen, and shewed ourselves so active, that the owner said he would rather have us than thirty of his own countrymen, which pleased the Governor, who was there, with almost the whole of the inhabitants and a band of music. After she was launched, the seamen amongst us helped to fit her out, being paid fifteen dollars per month, with provisions on board.

The governor had undertaken to write to the supreme governor in Santiago to plead the convicts' case. In doing so, he must have repeated the facts of their story: who they were, where they came from, and how they got there. We have no idea how what follows happened, but their story became news. The 9 May 1834 issue of the Chilean government newspaper *Araucano*[14] carried a report of the arrival in Valdivia on 9 March of ten men who said their ship 'had been lost on the open sea'. The men claimed to have been passengers and crew from an English brig, *Mary of Liverpool*, headed for Valparaiso. Their ship had hit a rock or a sandbank, they didn't know which, and they had taken to the ship's launch to save themselves. According to *Araucano*, the men's story was pretty implausible and 'orders were given to make a new and more rigorous investigation'.

---

14 The Spanish name for the Mapuche Indigenous people of Chile, who occupied a large area of central Chile.

What form this 'more rigorous investigation' took is not stated, but it elicited the information that the ten men were in fact criminals who had escaped from Van Diemen's Land. The *Araucano* report was carefully preserved by the British consul in Santiago and forwarded to Governor Arthur in Van Diemen's Land. This process will not have been quick (the report probably had to be sent to London first, before being passed on to Arthur), but it seems certain that by early 1835 the authorities in both Hobart and London knew exactly where to find the missing convicts.

Meanwhile, the governor ordered that the men be freed. However, he had a warning for Jimmy. Cheshire had asked the governor to protect him, because he was afraid Jimmy would kill him if the chance arose. 'I hope you in particular, Porter, will not molest him,' the governor warned. Jimmy's response was ominous. 'I made no answer,' he wrote.

———

The first couple of years in Chile appear to have been peaceful and fulfilling ones for the *Frederick* convicts—perhaps, for some, the happiest of their lives. According to Jimmy, five of them—John Barker, William Cheshire, James Leslie, Benjamin Russen and William Shiers—married local women, who bore them children. According to Jimmy, even the governor attended Barker's wedding.

This all sounds like one of Jimmy's more colourful stories, but there is independent evidence that he may have been telling the truth about the governor's appearance at Barker's wedding. In his scholarly book *La Sociedad en Chile austral antes de la colonización alemana* ('Southern Chilean Society before the German Colonisation'), the Benedictine monk Father Gabriel Guarda reports two of these marriages. According to Father Gabriel, on 25 August 1834, in Valdivia, John Barker married Doña Carlota Jiminez Puga. Father Gabriel also tells us that a John Leslie (or Lesley) Sutherland was married in Valdivia to Doña Juana Pinuer and Molina. This time there is no date given. The fact that the two wives were both accorded the title *doña* confirms that they were from respected families.[15] So Jimmy's claim that the governor attended the Barker wedding is at least plausible. As has been noted earlier, there was a fashion for high-born Chilean women to marry Europeans, and just about any European would do, even one on the run from the law. The fact that Barker's wedding took place almost exactly six months after the men arrived in Chile suggests that demand for marriageable Europeans must have well exceeded supply.

By all accounts, the men now settled down to something akin to normal life. Jimmy found work and lodgings with a local merchant, Don Lopez. Lopez treated him like family, and Jimmy rewarded him in his usual way, by taking another job.

Jimmy's narrative in his Norfolk Island journal continues with a series of highly improbable episodes in which he is

---

15 In Spanish culture, the civility *doña* is the feminine equivalent of *don*, an acknowledgement of distinction made famous by Cervantes' noble fool and hero Don Quixote.

the dashing hero. He leaves Lopez to act as bodyguard for a widow in danger; then he saves an Indian slave girl from her cruel mistress, namely the widow in question; he almost kills the widow after she attacks him with a knife; he singlehandedly defeats four armed soldiers who had come to kill him; he fights off a drunken Indian who had been paid by the soldiers to kill him; he pleads successfully for the Indian would-be assassin to be spared from being shot, after meeting the assassin's wife and young child and taking pity on them; and finally, his four soldier assailants confess that they were behind the whole plot to kill Jimmy and he pleads successfully for them to be freed also. Gratitude all round and warm words of praise for Jimmy the Hero.

After his adventures, whatever they may have been, Jimmy returned to Valdivia to work again with Don Lopez. Real trouble stayed away for almost a year. Then it arrived by sea. On 10 February 1835 the *Blonde*, a British frigate under the command of Commodore Mason, arrived at the Valdivia harbour entrance, undoubtedly in the wake of the *Araucano* revelations. In Jimmy's swashbuckling Norfolk Island account, the *Blonde* sent a small boat into the harbour. As it passed the outer fort guarding Valdivia, the fort gave it a shot across its bows from a 32-pounder, and the sailors beat a hasty retreat.

The *Blonde* moved out to sea and out of harm's way. However, after waiting four days at sea, she returned by night to Valdivia harbour with a letter for the governor. The governor responded to this by ordering the arrest of all ten convicts. They were duly locked up in the guardhouse. This, the governor explained, was for their own protection against any attempt by the British to nab them. The governor then asked them to translate Commodore Mason's letter to him. The letter said that Mason had heard that there were several Englishmen in Valdivia who had 'come to the coast in a clandestine manner'. Would the mysterious Englishmen like to come aboard the *Blonde* and explain themselves? Did the convicts want to do as Mason said? the governor asked. The response was loud, clear and predictable: 'No!' The governor then said he would ask Commodore Mason if he would like to come ashore, alone, and interview the men. Mason wasn't having any of this. He gave orders for the *Blonde* to sail for Valparaiso and the British naval base there. As soon as he was sure the danger had passed, the governor released all ten convicts. Normal life resumed.

———

To be entirely safe, the convicts still needed a favourable response to Governor Sanchez's petition to the supreme governor in Santiago, which had asked that the men be allowed to stay in Chile as free men. The response was a long time coming. Indians had captured the courier on his way back from Santiago, so it was said, and there was no way of knowing the supreme governor's verdict.

During this waiting period, the governorship of Valdivia Province changed hands. The kindly and sympathetic Sanchez returned to Santiago, where he promised he would look into the convicts' case and send word back to his successor. Before leaving, he explained the convicts' story to the new governor,[16] who agreed to continue the present freewheeling arrangements.

Soon after Sanchez left, the new governor struck. The convicts must all report daily at 6 p.m. to the Officer of the Guard. To the convicts it felt like Macquarie Harbour revisited. They discussed the new situation, and agreed that they would take the first opportunity to escape. That opportunity came when a large American brig, the *Ocean*, arrived at Valdivia under the command of Captain West. The brig was found to be carrying contraband and impounded. The convicts offered to help the captain recapture his ship by force and to sail it away with him. The captain agreed.

For two days the convicts waited. In that time West managed to raise £2000—a huge sum—in bond money and hand it over to the authorities. He was free to sail away. This he did, but not before three of the convicts—John Dady, John Fair and John Jones—managed to swim to the ship and board it. Three down, seven to go.

———

Three other convicts—John Barker, James Leslie and Benjamin Russen—had been working on an elaborate and temptingly seaworthy whaleboat intended for the governor's use. They finished it on a Saturday, and sailed off in it that night. Three more down, four to go.

———

16 Jimmy gives the new governor's name as Thomson, but that is about as reliable as his previous efforts.

Both the kindly Sanchez and his successor had warned that if any of the convicts escaped, those left behind could expect to suffer. This proved to be all too true. On the Sunday morning after the escape of Barker, Leslie and Russen in the governor's whaleboat, all four of the remaining convicts—Jimmy Porter, William Cheshire, Charles Lyon and William Shiers—were arrested and taken to prison, where they were chained together in pairs, Shiers with Jimmy, Lyon with Cheshire. Although they were now all prisoners together, Jimmy's feud with Cheshire continued. In his Norfolk Island journal he takes to referring to him as the Traitor Cheshire.

In Jimmy's account, they remained in chains for seven months. Then Jimmy saw a chance to escape, and took it. He slipped his chains, and was on the run for the better part of a week before he was captured and brought before the governor. The governor asked him why he had escaped. Jimmy claims to have responded: 'Two reasons I had for so doing: first, the cruel treatment and oppression of a Tyrant like yourself; secondly, with the hope of obtaining my liberty.'

If we are to believe Jimmy, the governor's response was brief and to the point: 'Take him to the Blacksmith's shop and see that a pair of Bar Irons is welded on his legs, and tomorrow I will order him to be shot in the Public square.'

So . . . death sentence number four, and counting.

Towards the morning a priest called Padre Rosa came to Jimmy's cell. He had not come to administer last rites, as Jimmy must have first thought, but rather to bring good news. Apparently a delegation of priests and 'females of distinction' had gone to the governor to plead for Jimmy's life. After a long argument, the governor relented. Jimmy was to be spared.

At about seven in the morning the governor appeared at Jimmy's cell and told the prisoner that he had his numerous friends to thank for the fact that he had avoided the fate he richly deserved for absconding. Jimmy responded:

> I informed him that I had thanked them in the strongest manner my grateful feeling would allow me, but not for him. I would not thank him for prolonging a life like mine, a life of misery, and in particular he, the Governor being the chief cause of it by his Oppression. He cast a fierce glance at me and then left me to myself.

In Jimmy's words, 'days, weeks, and months rolled on'. The fate of the convicts was finally settled by a new intervention by Commodore Mason and the *Blonde*. The four remaining convicts were told they would be taken that afternoon to the schooner *Basilisk*, which was then anchored in Valdivia harbour. The *Basilisk* was, in turn, the tender for the *Blonde*. The convicts boarded the *Basilisk*, which set sail for the British naval base in Valparaiso. When they reached Valparaiso they were informed that the *Blonde* had sailed on to Callao, the port of the Peruvian capital, Lima. The *Basilisk* finally caught up with the *Blonde* at Callao, and the four convicts were transferred to the frigate. They were promptly sent below decks and shackled.

While the *Blonde* was still riding at anchor in Callao harbour, Jimmy decided to seize his chance and escape. It was night, and everybody was supposed to be asleep. He slipped his chains and crept up onto the deck. He was caught by a marine before he could jump from the ship. How was the marine alerted? Cheshire and Lyon had rattled their chains to tell the guards that something was up. Of course.

After several more days at anchor in Callao, the *Blonde* sailed back to the British naval base at Valparaiso. The four prisoners were transferred to a warship, the 28-gun *North Star*, bound for England. In England they were transferred to the prison hulk *Leviathan* before being finally transferred to the *Sarah*, which had been chartered to transport convicts to Van Diemen's Land. There the four would be tried for piratically seizing the brig *Frederick*, a crime that carried a mandatory death sentence.

The *Sarah* arrived in Hobart on 29 March 1837, more than three years since the convicts had waved an unfond farewell to Macquarie Harbour. Their trial was scheduled to begin a month later, on 26 April, in Hobart Town.

At this point Jimmy and his three fellow prisoners might have reasonably concluded that they had a few weeks to wait for their trial, perhaps a day or two more to wait for a guilty verdict and the inevitable death sentence, then at best a few months before their appointment with the hangman. They were dead men.

Part 5

PRISONERS

Chapter 10

TRIAL

The trial of the four captured *Frederick* conspirators promised to be sensational, and it did not disappoint. William Cheshire, Charles Lyon, James Porter and William Shiers were charged with 'feloniously carrying away on the 13th of January 1834 the brig *Frederick*, Charles Taw master and belonging to Our Sovereign Lord the King, of an estimated value of £1200, from the high seas, to wit Macquarie Harbour on the Coast of Van Diemen's Land'.

The *Hobart Town Courier* reported that there were three counts in the indictment. The first charged the four with piracy, and the second with breaking their trust as sworn mariners, or mutiny. The third charge was the same as the second except that it did not state that Charles Taw, the master, had been confirmed in his position by the King. The convicts' conduct records are less wordy: all four were charged with 'piratically and feloniously seizing the brig *Frederick* from Macquarie Harbour 13th January 1834'. For the four men charged, all this play with words didn't matter much: all the charges carried a mandatory death sentence.

The trial began in the Supreme Court of the colony of Van Diemen's Land at 10 a.m. on Wednesday 26 April 1837. It was all over by seven that night. To put it mildly, the odds were stacked against the prisoners. They had no legal representation and conducted their own cross-examination of witnesses despite their lack of any legal training or professional advice. On the other side, no less weighty a personage than the solicitor general of the colony conducted the case for the prosecution. The judge was His Honour the Chief Justice, John Pedder, while the jury was entirely military. It speaks well for the four convicts that they appear to have been undaunted by all the flapping silk, quaint wigs and other legal trappings. The *Hobart Town Courier* went so far as to say that Jimmy Porter's cross-examination of witnesses was 'conducted with considerable acuteness'.

As is usual, witnesses for the prosecution were called first. David Hoy, master shipbuilder, was the first witness. He told the court he knew all of the prisoners well. William Shiers and William Cheshire had worked for him in the shipyard on Sarah Island, while Charles Lyon and James Porter were on the crew of the Macquarie Harbour pilot ship. So he was able to identify all four prisoners with complete confidence, and to give an accurate account of the role each had played in the seizure of the *Frederick*.

Hoy proceeded to deliver a dry, understated account of the events of the evening of 13 January 1834. There was little dispute as to the facts. Hoy's testimony is the backbone of Chapter 7 of this book, and the chapter reflects his matter-of-fact manner as he recalled what had happened.

Hoy was undoubtedly the Crown's star witness, and he was asked to go beyond the simple narrative of the seizure of the *Frederick*. He set before the court the precise nature of the ship's legal status, without which the charges would not stick. He explained that orders had been received to build the ship at Macquarie Harbour, with Hoy supervising its construction for the government. It was therefore the property of the King. Before the ship was stolen, Major Bailey,[1] the commandant of the Macquarie Harbour settlement, had ordered Captain Taw to take charge of the ship. Hoy had personally witnessed Bailey giving this instruction. Hoy had always understood that Taw was a North Briton and a subject of the King. So Taw was the lawful master of the *Frederick*, and disobeying his orders was mutiny. Finally, Hoy confirmed that the prisoners at the bar were all prisoners of the Crown at Macquarie Harbour before they absconded in the *Frederick*.

It looked like an open-and-shut case: the four men had been part of a gang that had organised a mutiny against the lawful command of Captain Taw and illegally seized the King's ship. Off to the gallows with them, then.

———————

The convicts had a simple objective: to escape hanging. There was no point arguing that they hadn't taken the ship and sailed

---

1   This is, among other things, an understandable misspelling by the *Hobart Town Courier*'s court reporter. On 11 March 1831 Major Perry Baylee (not Bailey) had become Sarah Island's last commandant, succeeding Captain Briggs.

it to Chile. Everyone knew they had, and everyone also knew that the penalty for piracy and mutiny was death by hanging. So instead the convicts set out to prove that they had behaved decently, humanely and, above all, non-violently, and that they were therefore worthy of the court's mercy.

William Shiers was the first to cross-examine a witness. He began by asking Hoy if he recalled that in the early stages of the takeover of the *Frederick* he (Shiers) had given Hoy a pocket compass and apologised for the fact that he was not able to give more. Shiers had also wrapped a bottle of whisky in a shirt and handed it to Hoy, urging him to keep it out of sight. Did Hoy agree that the convicts had given the shore party about 181 pounds of meat and 61 pounds of flour? They had also told the shore party that plenty of potatoes and cabbages could be found at the pilot's house. Finally, the shore party also received an iron pot, two or three tin pannikins, and an axe. Hoy agreed that all this was so.

Hoy had given evidence that during the takeover of the ship Shiers pointed a pistol at Hoy's head and threatened: 'We have got the vessel, and if you don't give yourself up, I will blow your brains out.' Shiers set out to argue that it wasn't a working pistol but a dummy made with a bar of iron. Hoy was indignant. The weapon presented by Shiers had every appearance of a pistol. Hoy did not think it was merely a bar of iron. He had reason to know that there were arms on board, and in any case prisoners were not allowed to carry arms. Furthermore, another of the convicts, John Barker, was 'a very ingenious man' and used to repair arms for the civilians and the military on the settlement: he might have made some kind of rough pistol out of old iron.

Charles Lyon then briefly cross-examined Hoy but, in the judgement of the *Hobart Town Courier*, 'elicited nothing of consequence'. He was followed by Jimmy Porter, who went to great lengths to establish the quantity of provisions on board the ship when it was seized, and the generosity of the convicts in willingly and voluntarily handing over half of them. He also drew out from Hoy the fact that when the convicts were leaving the men ashore, Hoy had said to him that the humanity and kindness the shore party had received from the prisoners was so great and unexpected that he could not forget it.

William Cheshire now took the floor. He spent his time seeking Hoy's agreement that he (Cheshire) had been a good and useful member of the shipbuilding team. Hoy was happy to concur. Hoy also agreed that he had told Cheshire that he would put in a good word for him when they reached Hobart, provided Cheshire continued his good behaviour.

One of the military jurors now had a question. Had Captain Taw *directed* the soldiers to go fishing? No, said Hoy, he had not. Taw had given them permission to leave the ship for an hour, but with strict instructions that they were to keep the ship in sight at all times. Finally, in response to a juror's question, it was established that the potato-gathering expedition of the previous day had not delayed the ship to the point of preventing them from leaving Macquarie Harbour. No, the wind had done that. The wind was 'not fair to carry [the *Frederick*] across the bar'.

At this point the convicts might have just about persuaded themselves that the trial wasn't going too badly. The prosecution's star witness had been far from hostile, and everybody seemed to agree that the convicts had behaved with restraint and humanity.

The next witness for the prosecution was James Tait, the acting mate of the *Frederick*. He added some details to Hoy's account of the seizure of the ship, but generally supported Hoy's version of events. He was first cross-examined by Charles Lyon. Tait was happy to confirm that Captain Taw was a habitual drunk and that his drunkenness led to incompetence. He had, for instance, cut the ship's lower rigging so badly that it was ruined. On the other hand, in Tait's opinion, Taw had been 'in a state of sobriety' on the day the ship was seized. (If so, it must have been a first.)

The court heard two more witnesses: the steward Nichols and the free man McFarlane. In the magisterial judgement of the *Hobart Town Courier*, 'they added nothing to the facts'. It was now the turn of the convicts to speak for themselves. None of them made any attempt to challenge the prosecution witnesses' version of events. In the words of the *Courier*:

> The prisoners in their defence, stated that they were compelled to join the mutiny, especially Lyon, who, it appears, was well acquainted with the navigation of that part of the coast; they laid considerable stress on the kindness they had shown Mr Hoy and his companions, particularly Shiers, who declared that his intention in rushing into the cabin

was to save Mr Hoy's life, by preventing any other person from taking it. Porter declared that the hardships they had endured, previously to their arrival at South America, were indescribable, and they all avowed that they had given themselves up to the Government there.

The jury retired at about 6 p.m. They were back in half an hour with a unanimous verdict: guilty as charged. The court adjourned for two days without passing sentence, though there could hardly be much doubt as to what the sentence would be. The case held the colony spellbound. As the *Courier* put it:

This case seems to have excited considerable interest; and the Court was excessively crowded during the whole trial. Lyon and Porter are intelligent and what may be termed 'smart' men; Shiers, apparently a quiet man, and Cheshire a weak lad. Porter was busily occupied in taking notes, of which he availed himself in his cross examinations.

So the trial ended, with the inevitable sentence still to come. But then something quite remarkable happened. As is so often the case, commercial expediency joined the side of the angels and galloped to the rescue of the convicts. The convicts' cause was popular with the public. Two local newspapers took it up.

The most spectacular intervention came on 5 May, with still no sentence passed by Chief Justice Pedder. An article appeared in the Hobart edition of the weekly newspaper *The Tasmanian*, buried in a long report on the activities of the Legislative Council. As it was published a mere nine days after the trial had concluded and, given the detailed and sophisticated arguments put forward, the anonymous author must have given the case a lot of thought before putting pen to paper. The article was not simply a plea for leniency out of regard for the convicts' non-violence and generosity. Instead it argued that the whole prosecution case was *wrong in law*. It was a clever legal argument, and the convicts had not used it in their defence nine days earlier. So *The Tasmanian*'s anonymous scribe must be credited with coming up with the winning defence.[2]

According to the newspaper, for charges of piracy and mutiny to stick, the prosecution needed to find its way around three points. First, piracy can only be committed on 'the high seas'. Second, for the seizure of a vessel to be a crime, the vessel itself must have proper legal status—it needs to be 'registered' if it is a merchant ship, or 'commissioned' or in possession of a 'warrant' if it is a King's ship, and the necessary paperwork to prove this point had never been put forward by the prosecution. Finally, for mutiny to be proven, the mutineers must have refused to obey the orders of a person duly authorised, and recognised as such in some tangible manner by the accused. In the view of the newspaper, the prosecution failed on all three points.

There could be no question that the *Frederick* had not been seized on the high seas. It was seized inside Macquarie Harbour. As any fool could tell, there was a ton of difference between

---

2   The article is reproduced as Appendix II of this book.

a harbour and the high seas. Furthermore, the *Frederick* had as yet no warrant or commission from the King, and had not been registered as a merchant vessel. It was therefore not a vessel in any legal sense, so anyone seizing it had not seized a vessel. Finally, there was no evidence that either Captain Taw or David Hoy were duly authorised to command the ship, and certainly no evidence that their authority was 'recognised' in some 'tangible manner' by the convicts. So the conviction of the prisoners was unsound, and hanging them would be a monstrous injustice.

What the men had done, according to *The Tasmanian*, was to steal a pile of wood belonging to the King. The old argument that if it looks like a duck, walks like a duck, and quacks like a duck, then it *is* a duck, had no place in the newspaper's case. The pile of timber stolen by the convicts may have looked like a brig, and even sailed like a (leaky) brig, but that still didn't make it a brig. For it to be a vessel in the legal sense it needed a warrant or registration papers, and there were none produced. For the convicts' actions to be deemed a mutiny, there had to be authorised persons to mutiny against, and the convicts had to recognise their authority. There were no such persons.

The Tasmanian went on to argue a more general point. When the system of transportation of convicts had been set up, the intention was that transportation itself was the punishment, in that it severed 'every tie of kin and country which endears the human being to life'. There had been no suggestion in the original legislation that there should be 'after punishment' on top of the transportation. However, a custom had grown whereby the original British sentence of 'transportation' had morphed into a sentence of slavery in a far-off land. This was a cruel and unjustified additional punishment. As the newspaper proclaimed, shouting its verdict in CAPITAL LETTERS:

Had such an announcement as this been made when the punishment of transportation was first adopted, the manly feeling of the British character would have risen in arms against such monstrously wicked cruelty! No! The transportation itself was the punishment—and dreadful indeed it is, easily pronounced as are the few words in which it is delivered; and UNJUSTLY, as in too many cases it is admitted to be pronounced.

We will quote the words of Governor King, and those of all his predecessors and all his successors, until the monstrous doctrine became established little by little—for how true is the French proverb *c'est le premier pas que coute* [roughly 'It's the first step that costs the most'] that independent of the sentenced punishment of transportation to the Antipodes, there was another punishment to be added, SLAVERY, to be rendered WORSE THAN DEATH!—'It is my business,' said the original Governors to the Crown prisoners, 'to keep you if I can, for you of course will get away if you can.'

The newspaper argued that, in the face of the unproclaimed and unlawful additional brutal punishment handed out to those sentenced to transportation, punishment which went way beyond the original intention of the court sentence, it was entirely reasonable for men to try to get away. These men and women had been sentenced to transportation. But that was their only sentence, and that was enough. They had not been sentenced to slavery.

———

While we have no way of knowing what went on in the minds of the lieutenant-governor and the chief justice, all the evidence points to the fact that *The Tasmanian*'s argument seriously rattled Justice Pedder. Four men had been tried in his court and found guilty of piracy. That carried a mandatory death penalty, so he would have little choice when passing sentence. But what if the men were hanged and it was subsequently found that the case against them was unsound? Might that make the chief justice a murderer in fact, if not in law? Pedder decided to keep pondering.

In 1837 the system of justice worked differently from today. It was possible, of course, for convicted men and women to appeal against their sentence. But they usually appealed for mercy or even a pardon, and their appeal went to the Executive Council of the colony rather than to a higher court located in a far-off Mother Country. If they wanted a verdict overturned, they could appeal to the House of Lords or to the colonial secretary in London, but that process was lengthy and inefficient and, in the case of the House of Lords, expensive. With the journey from Van Diemen's Land and back taking anything up to a year, a condemned man might be well and truly hanged before the colonial secretary had a chance to intervene. So an appeal to the colony's local Executive Council held out better prospects of success overturning a sentence.

The Executive Council, which effectively ruled the colony, consisted of the lieutenant-governor, the chief justice and various handpicked worthies from among its more prominent citizens. It is significant that the anonymous scribe in *The Tasmanian* directed his plea to 'Mr Kemp'. Anthony Fenn Kemp was a rich maverick who had just been reappointed magistrate by Lieutenant-Governor Sir John Franklin after quarrelling with Franklin's predecessor, George Arthur. Kemp was also a member of the Executive Council. *The Tasmanian* described him as someone who had served 'under all the Governors, from the first landing up to Governor Macquarie inclusive', and a close friend of 'Captain John Macarthur, the father and founder of the Australian Aristocracy'.[3]

In general, justice in the form of hanging in Van Diemen's Land in 1837 was dispensed with the least possible delay. Anyone sentenced to death had a life expectancy of months at the very best, and mere days if he or she was unlucky. However, the article in *The Tasmanian* and subsequent representations had clearly sowed seeds of doubt in the minds of the authorities, and they chose to leave the four men unhanged while they deliberated.

---

3   As there was, and is, no 'Australian aristocracy', this was a dubious accolade at best.

Meanwhile, the four convicted men were far from idle. Members of the Executive Council continued to agonise over their case. That gave the men time to look around for grounds to appeal. The article in *The Tasmanian* was a good starting point, and they were not without friends in the colony.

Chapter 11

APPEAL

An unexpected figure now moved to centre stage of the Hobart drama. The new arrival was G.K., the anonymous government clerk who had visited Sarah Island eleven times between 1822 and 1832 and who wrote so perceptively and movingly about the plight of the convicts incarcerated there. In his account of his entry into the Hobart fray, he says he received a message from Thomas Capon, the Hobart Town gaoler. The message came 'in early April of 1837', which means it was sent and acted on before the trial of the four convicts began on 26 April. The message was simple: a prisoner awaiting trial was asking to see G.K. The prisoner was Jimmy Porter.

G.K. had previously convinced himself that a message he deliberately failed to deliver had contributed to the decision to complete the *Frederick* at Sarah Island, forcing the ten convicts to remain behind and thus making possible the seizure of the brig. Thus G.K. saw himself as part of the conspiracy to steal the *Frederick*, though he was anxious to keep this explosive fact secret from his wife and the world in general. He was sympathetic to the convicts, and readily agreed to see Jimmy in Hobart Gaol. In G.K.'s words: 'Porter greets me with a friendly grin and a handshake that sends a chill down the spine. I do not have to ask. Porter knows exactly of my role in the conspiracy to build the *Frederick*. In his eyes I am one of them.'

Nevertheless, Jimmy's request came as a surprise. 'Sir,' said Jimmy, 'I want you to teach me to write! I want to write [my story] for myself.'

'Well,' G.K. replied, 'I will do what I can.'

———

G.K. dived into the task with gusto, visiting Jimmy 'every few days'. He concentrated on 'helping Porter to shape his sentences' as Jimmy set out his version of the seizure of the *Frederick* and the voyage to Chile. G.K. also brought Jimmy some books to read—Caesar's *Gallic Wars* (which served as a primer), and *Gulliver's Travels*, which Jimmy declared 'the best story he'd ever heard'. (Jimmy eventually made his way through the entire book.)

This process continued for a week or so until a second prisoner asked to see G.K.: this time it was William Shiers. As G.K. tells it: 'An hour of conversation with William Shiers is to produce a conviction in me about these fellows which will occupy me for the next two years, nearly all my spare waking hours, and indeed what working hours I am able to steal from the Treasury' [then G.K.'s employer].

Shiers was the first prisoner to take seriously the legal arguments put forward by *The Tasmanian*. As G.K. reports:

The appeal for clemency, to have the death sentence commuted to a further term of life transportation, is already in process but Shiers is not at all confident in its success and he proposes another line of appeal, not against the sentence but against the original charges of piracy and mutiny. Porter treats Shiers' idea with savage mockery and Shiers wants me to make some enquiry among the legal fraternity of my acquaintance to see if the appeal might have some substance.

G.K. sought out David Hoy, who by then had transferred to Port Arthur, where he enjoyed the title of acting master shipbuilder. Hoy told G.K. that he had spent the past two years in 'Napoleonic exile' on South Bruny Island building a lighthouse. He was inclined to think he had been sent there as punishment for his suspected complicity in the *Frederick* conspiracy. G.K. met Hoy at his private shipyard on Battery Point in Hobart, where the keen-eyed G.K. spotted several 'graduates' of Sarah Island. One of the ex-prisoners was effusive in his praise for Hoy and what he had learned from him. 'Best thing that ever happened to I,' said John Knight. 'Set for life, I be.'

Hoy turned out to be willing to join G.K. in helping the four convicts. He agreed that Shiers's wild scheme to challenge the charge of piracy might *just* succeed in a court of law, and offered to prepare a statement setting out the relevant maritime law. However, he also advised caution, particularly in revealing that he (Hoy) had agreed to help the defence team. 'I may be a liability if it is known,' he warned.

Hoy and G.K. agreed on a strategy well ahead of its time. In 1837 Van Diemen's Land was scarcely a democracy. It was ruled by an appointed governor supported by an appointed Executive Council, all of them answerable to a colonial secretary in London, half a world away. In the circumstances, local public opinion would seem to be unimportant at best, and irrelevant at worst. Hoy and G.K. agreed that the new lieutenant-governor, Sir John Franklin, was desperate to drum up a bit of public support. Franklin was a Royal Navy admiral and a renowned Arctic explorer. He was personally liked, particularly because his appointment ended the reign of the despotic and despised Governor Arthur.

Franklin's wife Lady Jane was regarded as 'difficult', in that she was a strong and determined woman who took up unpopular causes such as female convicts' rights.[4] Some of her unpopularity was beginning to rub off on Sir John. What he needed was a public relations coup. On the evidence of newspaper articles and letters it is clear that there was already plenty of support for the *Frederick* convicts, so here was an opportunity for Sir John to do well by doing good.

Hoy wrote a letter to the editor of *The Tasmanian*, and the newspaper published it. At Hoy's suggestion, G.K. began attending meetings of the Anti-Transportation League. As G.K. tells it: 'On my rather modest suggestion during one meeting, [the Anti-Transportation League] took up the cause of the

---

4   It is a measure of her 'difficulty' that her most prominent biography is titled *This Errant Lady*.

Frederick men.' So the first tentative rumblings of support for the four condemned convicts were beginning to show signs of swelling into a roar of popular outrage.

While all this was going on, Jimmy continued to write his story under G.K.'s tutelage. More than once, G.K. and Hoy had to dampen Jimmy's unquenchable desire for self-promotion. Whenever Jimmy tried to suggest in the journal that he had led or inspired or even encouraged his fellow convicts to take drastic steps to secure their freedom, a restraining hand was placed on his shoulder. 'You could hang for that,' his two muses warned him. The result was a longish document devoted to the singular cause of saving Jimmy from the hangman. It played down his role, and suggested he was an innocent dupe led astray by a bunch of hard men.

G.K. and Hoy, in their new capacity as public relations team for the defence, now had another idea. The new proprietor of the *Hobart Town Almanack* was William Gore Elliston. He had been a London theatrical entrepreneur, about as chancy a profession as exists on the planet, before moving to Hobart. He decided to apply his entrepreneurial talents to Van Diemen's Land by borrowing heavily to buy the most popular newspaper in the colony, the *Hobart Town Almanack and Van Diemen's Land Annual.* Now Elliston had an urgent problem. He desperately needed to get his hands on a shedload of cash to repay the massive loans he had undertaken to buy the newspaper. This could best be done through a swift surge in the paper's circulation. What better way to attract extra customers than with an exclusive rattling-good-yarn first-person true story, one that had already captured the public's imagination? The story also had the advantage of being set in Van Diemen's Land. Some of his readers might even know some of the central characters.

Jimmy completed the journal on 1 November 1837, and it was published in the 1838 edition of *Hobart Town Almanack and Van Diemen's Land Annual*. According to G.K., it was an instant sensation: 'It appealed to the readers, so Porter became for a time quite a celebrity.'

G.K. was certainly not taken in by Jimmy, nor did he wholeheartedly embrace the facts set down in the journal. 'I cannot of course vouch for its accuracy,' he wrote afterwards, 'and knowing James Porter a little I would doubt it entirely free of fabrication.' G.K. even attempted a little early-days psycho-analysis. 'In the months I listened to his tales of derring-do, James Porter displayed a characteristic I now understand to be *narcissism*. Nothing he did was ever considered bad or wrong.'

━━━ ━ ━

While all this was going on, the appeal process continued behind closed doors. These matters were normally settled within months or even weeks of a trial, but the four men's appeal remained undecided for more than two years, an incredibly long time between conviction and execution in the nineteenth century. Jimmy and his backers were optimistic. The final paragraph of Jimmy's Hobart journal spelled this out: 'We were found guilty and sentenced to be hanged; but which we have every reason to believe will be commuted to transportation for life.

And our case has gone home for the opinion of the English Judges.' It was dated: 'Gaol, Hobart, 1st November 1837'.

Despite the reference to English judges, there is no record of a formal appeal to the House of Lords in London. Jimmy's journal was sent to the colonial secretary together with a plea for clemency. It appears to have made it as far as the desk of Baron Glenelg, British Secretary of State for War and the Colonies from 1835 to 1839. It is certainly mentioned in the colonial secretary's correspondence archive, currently held in Hobart.

As it turned out, the convicts need not have bothered with London. Their fate was ultimately settled in Hobart, not as the result of merciful leanings on the part of the authorities, but because the authorities simply did not know what to do. Their ultimate treatment is quite a saga, and something of a legal mystery.

Begin by saying that on 26 April 1837 the four men were found guilty of 'piratically and feloniously seizing the brig *Frederick* from Macquarie Harbour [on] 13th January 1834', a charge that carried a mandatory death sentence. But Chief Justice Pedder did not don his black cap and deliver the inevitable sentence on the day of the hearing. Instead the court adjourned for two days. The adjournment was not to give Pedder time to ponder the appropriate sentence for the four men. According to the *Hobart Town Courier*, the court adjourned until the next case came before it: 'The trial of the murderers at Norfolk Plains is, we understand, to come on today [Friday 28 April, two days after the trial of the *Frederick* convicts].' In all the various writings, from G.K.'s diaries to Jimmy's journal, it is repeatedly stated that the men had been sentenced to hang, and that they were simply waiting in Hobart Gaol for their appointment with the hangman. Yet there is no reference to a death sentence in any of the four convicts' conduct records, nor can I find any mention of such a sentence in contemporary Tasmanian newspapers.

What we do know is that Chief Justice Pedder had doubts about the legality of the whole process. On 27 May 1839, more than two years after the trial and guilty verdict, he wrote a formal letter to Governor Franklin saying he had received contradictory legal advice on the question of whether Macquarie Harbour formed part of the 'high seas', so stealing a ship there might or might not be an act of piracy. The implication was clear: the conviction of the four men was unsound. Hanging them would therefore be unjust.

The governor now knew exactly what to do: the Executive Council met the next day and decided that the men should not hang. This piece of good news was kept back from the condemned men for another seven weeks. On 15 July 1839, two years and three months after their trial and conviction, the governor ruled that the four men should be transported to the Norfolk Island penal settlement. According to Jimmy: 'We never received any sentence from the court.' Even then, the men weren't told the full details of the governor's sentence.

So the PR campaign devised by G.K. and Hoy had succeeded brilliantly, if not completely. William Elliston had the circulation boost he needed to start paying off his debts. Sir John was a popular hero for righting an injustice. And the four men had been spared from hanging. Even Jimmy was grateful to the governor. He wrote later: 'Had not the Colony been under the Government of the humane Sir John Franklin I would not have been alive. Woe to us had the blood thirsty Arthur have ruled.' So Jimmy's fifth—and, the reader will be relieved to hear, final—death sentence had gone the way of the previous four.

Still, the four men remained prisoners. They might or might not have committed an act of piracy, but there was no dispute over the fact that they had stolen a pile of wood belonging to the King. The fact that the wood had been arranged in the form of the brig *Frederick* was neither here nor there. Stealing wood was a serious offence and merited serious punishment. Norfolk Island had a reputation for brutality almost as ferocious as the late and unlamented Sarah Island. So the governor's act of mercy, while welcome, had a sting.

It was only when the men reached Norfolk Island that they learned the details of their new sentence. It was another case of 'abandon hope, all ye who enter here'. The governor had ordered their transportation to the notorious penal settlement for life.

Chapter 12

NORFOLK ISLAND

Norfolk Island is a strange and haunted place. It is 1412 kilometres due east from the Australian coast, a volcanic rock jutting out of the Pacific Ocean. It is only 34.6 square kilometres in area, with a population in 2016 of 1748. In Jimmy Porter's day the population would have been pretty much the same, made up of 1200 convicts plus soldiers, other supervisors and a smattering of free men and women. Robert Hughes's superb 1986 book *The Fatal Shore* described the harsh conditions for convicts exiled to the island.

Norfolk Island has rich red soil, so it is good farming land. Its biggest problem—given that most of its supplies have to come by sea—has always been the lack of any proper port or harbour. Today there is a wharf of sorts called Kingston Jetty at Slaughter Bay on the southern coast, and another called Cascade Pier at Cascade Bay on the northeast side of the island. Neither wharf can accept cargo ships, and goods still have to be loaded into whaleboats and ferried ashore to the two jetties.

Today, the island is an external territory of the Commonwealth of Australia, and is run by an administrator appointed from Canberra. It had a brief period of independence, from 1979 to 2006, during which time it was a tax haven: residents paid no income tax. One of those residents was the international bestselling author Colleen McCullough (of *The Thorn Birds* fame), who moved there in the late 1970s and lived there until her death in 2015. This bold tax-free policy eventually and inevitably unravelled, and the island went bust. On 6 November 2010, Chief Minister David Buffett announced that the island would end its tax haven status in return for a bailout from the Australian government.

Visitors can prod around the convict ruins and explore the surviving history. However, tourism has never really caught on there, despite the much-improved airport and five flights a week from Auckland, Sydney and Brisbane. The island has some nice beaches, and the subtropical climate makes it a good place to spend a few lazy days. I doubt that anything quite so agreeable was enjoyed by Jimmy Porter and his fellow convicts.

———

Jimmy learned from day one that Norfolk Island deserved its reputation for harsh and mindless brutality. As he tells it:

> One Major Bumbry [Thomas Bunbury] was Commandant when I landed, and I saw a specimen of his cruelty the moment I landed. A man was being dragged before him, with irons on, he could scarce crawl in, and before he could

reach the office he [Bunbury] ordered him 50 lashes without even enquiring into the cause.

Bunbury lasted less than a year in the job, to be temporarily replaced by Thomas Ryan (whose name Jimmy spells as Rian), an altogether more sympathetic character. As Jimmy tells it:

He proved himself to be as much the father to the poor exiles as Bumbry did the Brute. Things went on very well at this time, and whenever Major Rian would converse with the prisoners he would inform them that one Captain Maconochie would soon make his appearance among us and that he was a better and kinder Commandant than himself.

Ryan forecast correctly. Alexander Maconochie was a prison reformer whose ideas have survived to this day. He first came into contact with the prison world in Hobart, where he had been assigned as Sir John Franklin's private secretary. Previously he had served with distinction in the Royal Navy, joining in 1803 as a midshipman, after which he moved up through the ranks until he was promoted to commander in 1815. His ship HMS *Calliope* fought in the British–American War of 1812–15, which ran alongside the Napoleonic Wars. He accompanied Sir John to Hobart, arriving in January 1837. One of his first actions was to write a damning report on prison discipline. The report found its way into the hands of Lord Russell, the British Home Secretary at the time, and is credited with marking the beginning of the end of the transportation system. He argued that, as cruelty debases both the victim and society, punishment should not be vindictive but should aim at the reform of the convict. This piece of pure common sense attracted huge criticism from the hangers and floggers who then dominated penal policy in Britain and elsewhere in the empire, to the point where Sir John felt compelled to fire his reform-minded secretary.

Maconochie languished in Hobart until the British Colonial Secretary Lord Normanby stepped in. Normanby had decided that reports of conditions on Norfolk Island were so disturbing that something must be done. What was needed was a new commandant more concerned with the moral welfare of the convicts than with either hanging them or stripping the flesh off their backs with a cat-o'-nine-tails. He chose Maconochie. The change on Norfolk Island was immediate. Let Jimmy tell it:

When he at last arrived, as proof of his Humanity the Gallows that used to stare us in the face was by his orders cut down and burned, a sure sign of a good feeling. His whole study has been to make us prisoners comfortable, and by Kind and Humane treatment to work a reformation in us. It had the desired effect on many refractory Characters that could not be ruled by harsh and cruel treatment. I speak for myself and five more young men that would rush upon the points of Bayonets to obtain our liberty previous to Captain Maconochie's arrival on the island. The Captain has placed dependence on us and we have proved to him and to all the officers on the island that our Commandant's

Humanity has brought us to a sense of our duty never to lose the only thing an exile doth possess, his word.

Thus you will find, my gentle reader, after all my trials and troubles I am safe moored at Norfolk Island, under a *Commandant* that alleviates the sufferings of the wretched Exile, and I now live in hopes by my good conduct of once more being a member of good Society.

Jimmy's Norfolk Island journal ends with these ingratiating words. He signs off with the word 'Concluded', then adds a scrawled signature: 'J^s Porter'. Being Jimmy, there is quite a flourish to the final 'r' in Porter.

———

Jimmy was true to the final words of his journal . . . and, later, true to his character. He had ended his Norfolk Island journal by saying he lived in hope that through good conduct he could be redeemed and rejoin society as a free man. In the vastly improved atmosphere of Norfolk Island under the command of Alexander Maconochie, Jimmy and his fellow convicts began the process of redeeming themselves.

In May of 1841, after less than two years on the island, Jimmy risked his life to take part in the rescue of some army officers whose boat had overturned in bad weather. For this act of bravery, his sentence was reduced from 'life' to fourteen years. Then in October 1842 the brig *Lunar*, standing off Norfolk Island in similarly foul seas, sent a distress signal saying it was desperately short of water. Jimmy volunteered to lead a rescue, and he and seven other convicts ferried 70 gallons (318 litres) of water through horrendous waves to relieve the ship. For this his sentence was reduced to seven years. Then, in October 1843, he was sent to Sydney with a recommendation that his sentence be 'remitted'.

However, a year later, for unexplained reasons, he was transferred to Newcastle, north of Sydney. In general, Newcastle functioned as a penal settlement for hardened criminals, so this transfer will have been punishment for some minor misdemeanour.

In Newcastle, Jimmy seems to have gone off the rails again. He was still under sentence, and therefore needed to watch his step. Instead he briefly disappeared, and on his return was sentenced to seven days' gaol for 'absenting'. Four months later, in February 1845, he received another seven days in gaol for 'disobedience'. Two months later he spent two weeks in gaol for 'assault'. That same month he reported an illicit still, an action that seems to have done him some good in the eyes of the authorities, because in June he was transferred back to Sydney. He worked for a while as a wardsman at the Hyde Park Barracks. Seven months later, on 22 January 1846, Jimmy achieved that highest of all goals for a convict still under sentence. He was granted a ticket of leave.

But true to form, Jimmy soon went off the rails yet again. On 11 February he was convicted of stealing, and gaoled for two months. His ticket of leave was cancelled. As part of his punishment he was sent back to Newcastle. Then he absconded, this time for good. He was last heard from sailing to New Zealand on the *Sir John Byng*, a 168-ton brig. We simply don't know whether he went as passenger or crew, or even stowed away. What happened next? He will have been in his mid-forties at the time, so he had plenty of life ahead of him. There is one final, laconic entry in his convict record book: in December 1853 he was officially struck off the records.

Chapter 13

WHATEVER
HAPPENED TO...

Research for this chapter did not come easily. Quite simply, a large number of the characters in this book had a strong and direct interest in disappearing from sight, and they have proved all too successful in doing so. Nevertheless, my excellent Chilean researcher Madeleine Blumer managed to track down some remarkable traces they left behind.

Whatever the difficulty of pinning down the final fate of my characters, the very happiest thing that can be said of them is that they all exited from this narrative as free men. As best as I can find out, this is what happened.

JIMMY PORTER

Did Jimmy Porter return to Chile, find Narcissa and their now adult son, and live happily ever after? Did he stay in New Zealand? Or did he return to England, or go somewhere completely new, like Greece or China? Whatever he did, he seems to have made pretty sure to leave no trace. Bear in mind that he was an absconding convict and liable to arrest if he was caught and identified. Having been grabbed once in Chile and hauled back as a prisoner to Van Diemen's Land, he would certainly have been anxious to avoid making that mistake again. So he is bound to have covered his tracks as best he could. If that is what he did, then his efforts have well and truly succeeded.

On my behalf, Madeleine Blumer pursued the name Porter through Chilean census data, genealogical texts and even Facebook. (For example, she wrote to everybody in Chile on Facebook whose surname or middle name was Porter.) There turned out to be several tribes of Porters in Chile. Madeleine found that a George (or Jorge) Porter had been married to a Mariana Wilkinson, with whom he had a son, Guillermo Porter Wilkinson. Guillermo married Catalina de los Santos in Valdivia in 1863. Was George the long-abandoned son of Jimmy's marriage to Narcissa? Was Jimmy there, on the groom's side of the aisle, to see his grandson married? Sadly not, as it turned out. George Porter arrived in Chile in 1807 from Strabane in Northern Ireland, and was entirely unconnected with Jimmy.

While researching, Madeleine spoke to one of George Porter's grandsons, who knew of another Porter family living in or near Concepción in central-southern Chile, between Valparaiso and Valdivia. That sounded promising, but at the time of writing this family was proving elusive.

If Jimmy did return, what might he have found in Chile? Would Narcissa have waited for him? Or did she find some way to remarry and build a second life? Despite Madeleine's diligent search through old records, no authoritative answers are forthcoming.

The story of the *Frederick* and its convict crew is comparatively well known in Chile, particularly in the area around Valdivia, where it has become part of local folk history and legend. The story is usually referred to as *Los evadidos de Tasmania* ('The escapees from Tasmania'). In Madeleine's words: 'Basically it's the same adventure that Jimmy describes in his journal about his second arrival in Chile in 1834, after the voyage of the *Frederick*.' Madeleine tells me there are many versions of the story (she has read at least ten), including some that go on to remind us that Jimmy Porter had a wife and son waiting for him in Chile, and that he might well have rejoined them there. And there are those who see this as a real possibility.

The Chilean novelist and historian Fernando Lizama-Murphy—a Chilean-Irish name if ever I heard one—published a brief but well-researched account under the title *James Porter, el bandido enamorado* ('James Porter: the bandit in love'). It is readily available. Anyone with a smattering of Spanish can read it at fernandolizamamurphy.com/2016/07/23/james-porter-el-bandido-enamorado. Señor Lizama-Murphy begins his story with a slightly nervous assertion: 'Many Valdivians still think this story is a legend, but I assure you that most of it is true.' He concludes his account with the suggestion that Jimmy may have made it back to Chile and died in Valparaiso or Valdivia, having been reunited with his Chilean family. So that happy ending has at least one thoughtful and erudite supporter in Chile.

Much as I would like to end this story on a high note and endorse Lizama-Murphy's conclusion, I can't. It seems to me that Jimmy's stated imperative throughout his life was to live as a free man. If he returned to Chile and Narcissa, his chances of being caught would have been intolerably high.

I doubt he would have stayed in New Zealand, then a British colony and too close to Australia for comfort. He might have picked up work in a ship's crew, maybe even on a whaler, which could have taken him back to Chile. But it's my guess that he headed off to somewhere unpredictable, like Japan or Russia. He might even have headed for America, where there was little love for the British and few questions were asked of strangers. Perhaps he regularly exchanged Christmas cards with John Barker, James Leslie or Benjamin Russen, who invited him to join them in the West Indies.

We will probably never know.

THE OTHER *FREDERICK* CONVICTS

William Cheshire, **Charles Lyon** and **William Shiers** were all sent to Norfolk Island with Jimmy Porter. Jimmy continued his feud with Cheshire to the bitter end. He had blamed Cheshire for falsely accusing him of plotting a mutiny on the voyage from England. He also wrote that Cheshire had tried to incriminate him again when they reached Hobart. Jimmy recounts improbable tales of magistrates and other gentlemen nodding in solemn and sympathetic agreement as Jimmy unfolds his tale of treachery and woe. It all strikes me as paranoid nonsense, and I have generally ignored it in the narrative.

There is a legend surrounding the fate of Charles Lyon that is widely believed but almost certainly false. While he was on Norfolk Island, he is said to have been one of the party of six convicts, including two convicts from Van Diemen's Land, sent in a rowboat to collect some soldiers on a hunting and fishing trip to Phillip Island. Choosing Lyon for this job would make sense. He was an experienced seaman, and Phillip Island, a rocky outcrop about 6 kilometres south of Norfolk Island, was well within his capabilities. But instead of simply picking up the soldiers and rowing back to the main island, the convicts stole the boat and set off into the Pacific. Their fate is unknown, but as the nearest mainland was more than 1400 kilometres away, into wind, their chances of survival in an open rowboat over such a distance were slim. If Lyon was indeed among them, he will have drowned with the rest of them.

A vastly more plausible story says that Lyon and Cheshire were sent back to Van Diemen's Land after they were caught trying to build an illicit boat to escape from Norfolk Island. They must have stayed out of trouble back in Hobart, because both received pardons.

There is a final snippet of information about Cheshire. The 21-ton schooner *Trumpeter*, a boat he had built at Surveyors Bay on the Huon River in 1851, became stranded while heavily laden with timber at Browns River, south of Hobart, on the night of 26 February 1854. Two of those aboard managed to struggle ashore, but Cheshire and another drowned.

Like Jimmy, William Shiers was sent back to New South Wales from Norfolk Island. In New South Wales he distinguished himself by helping to rescue the schooner *Patterson* from deadly danger. For this he received a full pardon, and was henceforward a free man.

Both Shiers and Cheshire are among the five convicts named by Jimmy as marrying Chilean brides. There is no record of either man ever returning to Chile to reclaim his bride and family. According to Richard Davey, the author of the excellent play *The Ship that Never Was*, descendants of Shiers now live in Darwin, Australia. One of those descendants, Wally Shiers, was a mechanic aboard Ross and Keith Smith's Vickers Vimy aircraft on their historic first flight from London to Australia in 1919. Cheshire is also said to have descendants still living in Australia.

John Dady, **John Fair** and **John Jones** had swum for it back in Valdivia harbour, and climbed aboard the American brig *Ocean*, where the captain agreed they could stay. That is the last anyone heard of them. The highest probability is that they finished up in the United States, where they will have presumably changed their names and disappeared into the no-questions-asked polyglot throng that was America in the mid-nineteenth century.

John Barker, **James Leslie** and **Benjamin Russen** escaped from Valdivia in the governor's stolen whaleboat. Nothing is known about them beyond the fact that they were seen alive in Jamaica three years later. If they made it to the West Indies in the stolen boat, they must have rounded Cape Horn in it, quite a feat. All three are named by Jimmy as having married Chilean brides who bore them children. They may have returned to Chile to support their families, but somehow I doubt it.

THE GOOD GUYS

David Hoy went from strength to strength. After his two-year 'exile' building a lighthouse on South Bruny Island, he was recalled to the mainland and became master shipbuilder, using convict labour, at the Port Arthur penal settlement. He also set up his own shipyard in Hobart, and at 49 married Janet Cameron. He lived to the age of 70, and died in Hobart a very wealthy man.

Alexander Maconochie returned to England in 1844 after transforming the penal settlement on Norfolk Island. In England he wrote a hugely influential book setting out his ideas for penal reform. In 1849 he accepted the job of governor of the new Birmingham prison, where he set about putting his liberal ideas into effect. A man ahead of his time, he faced a storm of criticism from prison officers, supervisors and the police, as well as from newspapers and parliamentarians. In the end, they won: he was sacked. He remained an influential writer and thinker on prison reform.

Immediately after Maconochie's departure from Norfolk Island, the settlement reverted to the old ways of terror and cruelty, which continued until it was closed on 5 May 1855. But Maconochie may have had the last laugh. Some 1400 convicts 'graduated' from his prison on Norfolk Island, and very few reoffended. None of his predecessors or successors could make the same claim for the convicts they oversaw. He is known today as the 'father of parole'.

THE PENAL SETTLEMENTS

Norfolk Island functioned as a penal settlement from the very beginning of Australian colonisation. Sydney was established on 26 January 1788, and on 6 March of the same year Philip Gidley King arrived on Norfolk Island with fifteen convicts and six soldiers. Six years later, Francis Grose,[5] then lieutenant-governor of New South Wales, proposed to close it. In his view, it was too remote and too expensive to maintain. However, it continued to function undisturbed until 1805, when some of the convicts were returned to Sydney. By 1813 it had closed down. All the buildings were deliberately destroyed, and it was left bare.

In 1824, the British government ordered the governor of New South Wales Sir Thomas Brisbane to reopen Norfolk Island as a prison for the 'worst of the worst': reoffenders and those who had been spared from hanging on condition that they be transported to a remote penal settlement for life. The British wanted Norfolk Island to be another tough regime along the lines of Sarah Island, with generous servings of hangings and floggings. As with Sarah Island, the designation 'worst of the worst' turned out to be hypocritical claptrap. More than half

---

5   No relation, I'm happy to reveal!

the prisoners sent to Norfolk Island were not reoffenders at all, and only 15 per cent were sent there as a reprieve for a death sentence. As with Sarah Island, it was simply a place to send awkward prisoners when the authorities took a dislike to them. The majority of prisoners on Norfolk Island had been convicted of non-violent crimes, mostly property offences.

As transportation began to wind down generally in the mid-nineteenth century, Norfolk Island was again seen as too remote and difficult. It was again abandoned: the last convicts on the island were transferred to Van Diemen's Land in 1855. What happened then was a triumph for Admiral Sir Fairfax Moresby.[6] The British had known since 1814 that the *Bounty* mutineers had settled on the Pitcairn Islands. However, of the original mutineers only John Adams remained alive in 1814, so there was little point in sending a special expedition to drag him back to England just to hang him, and he was granted amnesty. He died in 1829, on Pitcairn.

While he was commander-in-chief of Pacific Station, Valparaiso, from 1850 to 1853, Sir Fairfax Moresby visited the Pitcairn Islands twice. He was much impressed by George

---

6   My wife's middle name is Moresby, and she comes from a long line of British Navy officers, including two admirals named Moresby. Her great-great-grandfather was Rear Admiral Sir Fairfax Moresby, and Port Moresby was named after his son, Admiral John Moresby. Sir Fairfax is revered on Norfolk Island. On the strength of the Moresby name, my wife and I were treated like VIPs when we visited, and invited to dinner at Government House. We were also introduced to the chief minister, who greeted us in shorts and an old T-shirt while carrying out his day job running the local garden centre.

Hunn Nobbs, who functioned as a kind of island chieftain. So impressed was Sir Fairfax by Nobbs that he personally paid to send him to England, where he was ordained by the Archbishop of Canterbury and met Queen Victoria. He also met and impressed a large circle of influential people in London before returning to Pitcairn, this time as an ordained minister and official spiritual leader. As a result of Sir Fairfax's generosity and Nobbs's charisma, the Pitcairn Islanders now had a lot of friends in high places in London.

By the mid-nineteenth century the Pitcairn community had grown to the point where the islands were not big enough to support them. Something had to give. Sir Fairfax helped to persuade the British government that the Pitcairn Islanders should simply be given the newly emptied Norfolk Island. He also facilitated their transfer from Pitcairn to Norfolk. On 3 May 1856 the entire population of the Pitcairn Islands, all 193 of them, set off in the *Morayshire* for Norfolk Island. They landed five weeks later, and quickly occupied the empty buildings and farms.[7] Their descendants are the elite of today's Norfolk Island population. There were few family names. The original *Bounty* mutineers had founded dynasties named Adams, Christian, McCoy, Quintal and Young. The very few outsiders who had made their way to Pitcairn added three more dynasties: Nobbs, Buffett and Evans. These eight family names are still revered on Norfolk Island today.

---

7   Some of them suffered from migrant's remorse, and within seven years 44 of them returned to Pitcairn. The returnees formed the basis of the current Pitcairn community.

Sarah Island, as we have seen, ceased to function as a penal settlement in 1833. It was tentatively revived in 1846–47 as a probation station for convicts sent there to cut timber, but this was not a huge success and it was again abandoned. The various mining rushes brought sporadic development to the west coast of Tasmania, and the miners took to picking apart the various brick buildings on the island and using the bricks to build their houses. Thus the substantial buildings on Sarah Island were slowly whittled away, to the point where they have almost entirely disappeared.

Towards the end of the nineteenth century, the Union Steam Ship Company leased the entire island, and promoted it as a good place for picnics. The island was taken over as a tourist reserve by the Tasmanian government in 1926, and in 1971 Sarah and Grummet islands were declared historic sites. Today they form part of the Tasmanian Wilderness World Heritage Area. Nobody lives on Sarah Island today, and the island is simply a tourist site. It is still possible to see remnants of the convict era in the form of the old penitentiary, some sunken logs that once functioned as boat slips, and some foundations. The rest has either rotted away or been stolen.

The nearest population centre is the village of Strahan, on the northern mainland shore of Macquarie Harbour. From there visitors can take a cruise on the Gordon River, fish, go for walks or simply laze about. The river cruises usually include a visit to Sarah Island, where the tourist has a choice of either following a guide or taking the self-guided walking tour while clutching an annotated map. The island is quite small: an hour is plenty of time for the self-guided tour.

Anyone visiting Strahan should be sure to include one of the daily performances of *The Ship that Never Was*, which is now Australia's longest-running play. It was first performed in 1984; the current season opened in January 1994, and the play has been running continuously ever since. It tells the story of the seizing of the *Frederick* and is great fun, with plenty of audience participation. 'Jimmy', ever the partisan, even requires the audience to hiss and boo whenever the name Cheshire is mentioned. Well, why not?

THE BRIG *FREDERICK*

After the convicts sighted the shore of Chile in February 1834, they simply abandoned the **Frederick**. The brig was allowed to sink to the bottom of the Pacific Ocean. It went down some 40 miles (64 kilometres) off the Chilean coast, probably near the mouth of the Bueno River. This is not far from the Peru–Chile Trench, a huge valley in the floor of the Pacific Ocean which can sometimes go as deep as 8000 metres. The water off Rio Bueno is anywhere between 500 metres and 2000 metres deep. So the wreck is well beyond the reach of scuba divers and has never been recovered or even seen. Given that it was built with Huon pine timber, it is probably still pretty much intact even after almost 200 years.

APPENDIX I

This is a reproduction of the original document chartering the *Asia* to take Jimmy and 249 other convicts to Van Diemen's Land. Naturally, the document was handwritten but in something akin to copperplate writing. I have reproduced it using Lucida Calligraphy typeface, the nearest I could find to the original. The reader will quickly discover that the charter was a straightforward commercial transaction. Notice that *ownership* of the convicts and their future labour passes to the shipbroker Joseph Lachlan, on the understanding that Lachlan will ensure that the convicts are delivered to New South Wales and that, once they are there, this ownership will pass to Governor Brisbane.

To all to whom these presents shall come Joseph Lachlan of Great Alie Street Goodmans Fields in the county of Middlesex Ship Broker Sends Greeting.

Whereas in and by certain indentures bearing date the twenty sixth day of July instant made between Thomas Shelton of the Sessions house in the City of London Esquire of the one part and the said Joseph Lachlan of the other part Reciting the convictions sentences and orders of transportation of the several convicts named or contained in the List or Schedule hereunto annexed And also reciting that His Majesty by his Royal Sign Manual bearing date the twenty-sixth day of April last had been pleased to give directions for the transportation of the said Convicts and had graciously thought fit to authorize and empower the said Thomas Shelton to make a Contract or Contracts with any fit person or persons for the effectual transportation of the said Convicts and to take security for the person or persons so contracting for the effectual transportation of them pursuant to the sentences and orders in the said Indentures recited concerning them respectively It is witnessed that the said Thomas Shelton by virtue of such power and authority and consideration of the Contracts and Agreements of the said Joseph Lachlan therein mentioned and of the securities given by him the said Joseph Lachlan by Bonds or Writings Obligatory bearing even date with the said Indentures for the effectual performance thereof did contract with the said Joseph Lachlan he being a fit person for the performance of the transportation of the said Convicts And further reciting that the said Joseph Lachlan in consideration of the property which he the said Joseph Lachlan his Executors Administrators and Assigns would have in the service of the said convicts for and during the remainder of the terms of their transportation and for divers other

good causes and considerations him thereunto moving
Did covenant contract with and agree to and with the
said Thomas Shelton that he the said Joseph Lachlan his
Executors Administrators or Assigns should and would
forthwith take and receive the said Convicts and transport
them or cause them to be transported effectually as soon
as conveniently might be to the Coast of New South Wales
or some one or other of the Islands adjacent pursuant
to the sentences and orders concerning them in the said
Indentures mentioned and should and would procure such
evidence as the nature of the case would admit of the
landing there of the said convicts (death or casualties by
sea excepted) and produce the same to whom it might
concern when lawfully called upon and should not nor
would by the wilful default of him the said Joseph Lachlan
his Executors Administrators or Assigns suffer the said
Convicts or any or either of them to return to Great
Britain or Ireland during the terms for which they were
respectively ordered to be transported the dates and terms
of which said sentences are mentioned and set forth in
this List or Schedule hereunto annexed And Whereas the
said Joseph Lachlan hath taken and received the said
Convicts on board a certain ship or vessel called the
"Asia" of which James Landsay is Master and Commander
which said Ship or Vessel is now lying at Woolwich bound
to New South Wales aforesaid in order to transport the
said Convicts pursuant to their said respective sentences
and orders Now Know Ye that the said Joseph Lachlan

*for and in consideration of the sum of Five Shillings
in hand at or before the sealing and delivery of these
presents the Receipt whereof the said Joseph Lachlan doth
hereby acknowledge and for divers other good causes
and valuable considerations him thereunto moving Hath
bargained sold assigned transferred and set over and
by these presents Doth bargain sell assign transfer and
set over unto His Excellency Major General Sir Thomas
Brisbane Knight Commander of the Bath and Governor
in Chief of the Territory of New South Wales and Islands
adjacent All his Right*

*Whereas Daniel Denysson Esquire, His majesty's Fiscal in
this Settlement of the Cape of Good Hope, has reported to
me that the Convict William Paris in his custody has been
sentenced by the Board of Landdrost and Heemadon of
the Cape District to Transportation to New South Wales
or one other of the Islands adjacent for the Term stated
in his Sentence, an authenticated Translation of which
Sentence fiatted by me is forwarded to His Excellency the
Governor of New South Wales and whereas the Convict
Ship Asia, James Lindzee Master, is now lying in Table
Bay bound to New South Wales aforesaid, on board which
it is fitting and expedient the aforesaid Convict should be
placed and secured in pursuance of his sentence.*

*These are therefore to require and command the said
J. Lindzee commanding the Convict Ship Asia to receive
on board the said Ship and Keep in due Security for*

conveyance to New South Wales the said Convict William Paris for which purpose this Warrant given under my hand and seal shall be to him the said J. Lindzee a Sufficient Warrant and Authority.

Dated at the Cape of Good Hope this Twenty Sixth day of November 1800 and Twenty Three.

By His Excellency's Command

Charles Somerset

APPENDIX II

Here is the full text of the article that appeared in the 5 May 1837 edition of *The Tasmanian (Hobart Town)* setting out the legal argument refuting the charges of piracy and mutiny against Porter, Lyon, Cheshire and Shiers. The article is unsigned. It also includes musings about the purposes of transportation, and the inhumanity and possible illegality of the harsh regime imposed on the convicts.

Four men, prisoners of the Crown, were found guilty of piracy last week. The offence was in carrying off a vessel, or rather (as one of them in his defence objected to the charge of carrying off the Brig *Frederick*) a quantity of wood and other materials so fastened as to possess the means of becoming a brig—but possessing no one constituent, necessary to justify those materials being then so called.

Of this offence the jury found them guilty, and but for the careful, humane, and most praiseworthy consideration of the Chief Justice Pedder, they would have received sentence of death. That that last terrible judgment of the law would have been carried into effect under all the circumstances for such an offence, even had it been committed as it was charged to have been, which it was not, none who have seen or has heard of Sir John Franklin venture for a moment to apprehend.

Before we proceed to offer a few, and but a few, observations upon this affair, we wish to draw attention to what was the original 'intent and purpose' of 'transportation,' and what was the conduct of the first Governors of these Colonies towards those whom the custody of the unhappy persons subjected to that operation of the law, was confided.

In the accuracy of what we are about to state, we appeal to Mr. Kemp, who is, we believe, since the death of his old friend and brother officer, Captain John Macarthur, the father and founder of the Australian Aristocracy; the father of the Colonies, if not of both Colonies, certainly of this.[8] Mr. Kemp, when a Captain in the 102nd regiment, filled the important offices, and it is only justice to him to state with great honour and credit, of Commandant at the most important stations in both Colonies.

---

8   The two colonies in question were New South Wales and Van Diemen's Land.

He served, we believe, under all the Governors, from the first landing up to General Macquarie[9] inclusive. Up to the removal of that ever-lamented and revered man, what was the principle [*sic*] feature of transportation? Those who were subjected to that of itself severe punishment, severing asunder as it does, every tie of kin and country which endears the human being to life, was sentenced as at present, to 'transportation beyond the seas'—those were and are the precise words of the sentence. That sentence so passed was carried into effect, but the punishment was considered to be, as the sentence conveyed, the transportation.

There was no after punishment to be inflicted by construction of law, or by collateral enactments made to evade the shock which humanity would have received at the time when the punishment of transportation was first adopted, had it been accompanied by a denouncement that it was a consignment to SLAVERY of the most heart-cutting character, 'worse than death itself' as it is now avowed from the Bench to be; and this, no matter what might be the nominal period of endurance: 'FOR LIFE, and as far as possible, upon the after generation beyond the grave.'

Had such an announcement as this been made when the punishment of transportation was first

---

9   This toadying nonsense is also factually incorrect. Macquarie was famously the first *civilian* governor of New South Wales, following four navy captains and two disastrous lieutenant-governors who were both army majors.

adopted, the manly feeling of the British character would have risen in arms against such monstrously wicked cruelty! No! The transportation itself was the punishment—and dreadful indeed it is, easily pronounced as are the few words in which it is delivered; and UNJUSTLY, as in too many cases it is admitted to be pronounced. And how did the Governors, who were the first Administrators of that punishment in these Colonies, consider themselves bound, in common fairness, to act towards those who were subjected to their 'Gaolorship', for such at the very best is the Government of a 'Penal Settlement?'

We will quote the words of Governor King, (words used by all his predecessors and his successors, up to the excellent Macquarie) that Governor being as is well known as rigid a disciplinarian as ever trod the quarter deck, yet withal with a heart too kindly to add gall to wormwood—what were his words and those of all his predecessors and all his successors, until the monstrous doctrine became established little by little—for how true is the French proverb *c'est le premier pas que coute* [roughly 'It's the first step that costs the most'] that independent of the sentenced punishment of transportation to the Antipodes, there was another punishment to be added, SLAVERY, to be rendered WORSE THAN DEATH!—'It is my business,' said the original Governors to the Crown prisoners, 'to keep you if I can, for you of course will get away if you can.'

We appeal to Mr. Kemp, and to all the original Colonists of the olden time, whether this was not the relative compact between Governor and prisoner? What is it now? The miserable wretch undergoing 'slavery worse than death' who should give way to the first impulse of his nature—that love of liberty, (that first and greatest of blessings) inherent to man, is to suffer death, for obeying that impulse, injuring no human being by that giving way! What is not the exquisite cruelty of this injustice, of thus indicting by man over his fellow-man, the last terrible punishment which man possesses the power of inflicting over his fellow, for thus giving way to the first impulse of his nature—for complying with that principle instinctively implanted in all animated nature from the first to the last in the scale—the love of liberty! Throughout the whole of that scale, man is the only animal in whom the love of torturing its kind seems to be such a source of delight, that to invent the best means of gratifying it is absolutely rendered into a science, to which a denomination is affixed—PRISON DISCIPLINE!

Let us now look at the particular circumstances of the case before us. Four men are charged with mutiny and piracy—crimes punishable, and we believe always, with death. There are three 'essentials' to these crimes: first, a ship, or vessel, properly so called; second, persons duly authorized in command, that authority recognized in some tangible manner by those on board; third, the crime of 'piracy' as so distinguished by law, can only be committed on 'the high seas.' Let us see how far any of these essentials are comprehended in the case under consideration.

First, the 'vessel' charged to have been piratically carried away possessed no one attribute to bring her within the legal extent of that term. There are many essentials thereto. A register of a merchant ship—a commission, or a warrant of some sort for a King's vessel—in a word, some distinguishing character of such a nature as shall bring her within the meaning of the term. Did the floating bundle of materials in this case so consist? The very opposite would seem to be the fact. The hull of a vessel, certainly with temporary equipment to enable her to be brought to the place where the real equipment has to take place, was put in motion, and was afterwards carried away by the accused (from whence we shall see by and by) previous to her being so equipped, established, registered, warranted, or in some other way rendered a ship or vessel, properly so called, within the meaning of the legal extent of the term 'piracy.' That which the accused took away was, in fact, as far as a legal offence goes, a mere bundle of materials of various descriptions.

Was there the next 'essential,' a person duly authorized, convinced, recognized as such in some tangible manner by the accused? Nothing of the sort. The evidence went to show that some persons, named Taw and Hoy, were on board—but what was the nature of their authority, or how recognized by the accused, there was not (we refer to the reports in the newspapers, which we suppose to be correct) one tittle of evidence. Thus much for two 'essentials' to the crime of piracy.

The third, that it should be committed on the 'high seas,' was not only not proved, but the very contrary was. The witnesses all deposed to the capture of the 'bundle of materials' called the *Frederick*, within the 'gates' of Macquarie Harbour—in the very harbour itself. Commanders of ships are vested with very large powers, but they are limited expressly to the time when their vessels are 'on the seas,' and have not the law to protect them. The very moment the anchor falls in a harbour, that very moment the powers possessed at sea cease and determine.

What then is the nature of the offence, which at the very utmost, these men could have been legally charged with, the stealing that bundle of materials for the purpose of making their escape from slavery. And here we entreat of the reader to divest himself (if possible) of all that hateful feeling arising from the fact of the enslaved condition of these miserable men. We ask of the reader in common candour to put away (if he can) from his mind reference of any sort to any other consideration than the mere abstract question of piracy. Let him not mix up with it any reference to the escape of the accused, because that it is a matter wholly foreign to the charge of piracy, provided for by other laws made expressly for the purpose, and whether rightfully or wrongfully made, quite strong enough for the purpose intended.

Let us illustrate this by supposing that a transport ship, on the passage out from England, was to be captured by a combined movement of the free sailors and the Crown prisoners; it is perfectly clear that the law would make no distinction in the offence between the two classes of men, who would be in one and the same class as offenders in the capture of the ship. They would be all equally mutineers and pirates, with which the freedom of the one, or the bondage of the other could not have had the slightest to do. So in the present case. Had the soldiers joined the prisoners, the offence of taking away the 'bundle of materials' would have been one and the same in all, neither diminished as to the soldiers that they were free, nor added to as to the prisoners that they were bond. The crime, be it what it may, in law, would have been the same!

Of what then have these men been guilty? That obeying the first impulse of human nature, which we commenced with referring to, they endeavoured to escape from slavery! That in that endeavour they not only committed no enormity of any, the slightest description—not even the breath of personal violence to any human being—but on the contrary, they exhibited so much forbearance in the manner in which they effected the purpose to which every feeling inherent to man so strongly induced them, that the people they put on shore expressed themselves, according to their own evidence, in the warmest terms of gratitude! Is there then in any one act of their proceeding, any one feature deserving that last of punishments which man can inflict upon his fellow man—DEATH!

We could add many more arguments to those which we now offer upon this distressing subject—we shall however add only one, but which one involves considerations of such great importance that we are convinced they must have escaped the notice of the Chief Justice, or His Honor would assuredly have bestowed upon them his attention. We approach it with reluctance, for reasons that will be readily understood, when the occurrences of the Session are recollected. The Criminal Court here is established by an Act of Parliament, by virtue of which its proceedings take place. There are two Judges, but there is only one Criminal

Court. Its sitting was by one of those Judges solemnly adjourned to a day certain.

Up to that day the Criminal Judicature was asleep, nor do we know of any authority which could awaken it until the time fixed but the actual dissolution of the Court itself, and the establishment by law of another. Yet did it awaken before the day to which it had solemnly adjourned, and proceeded to action. Repeat, we approach this point, under the circumstances, with reluctance, and we shall not further touch it, than to suggest that in the absence of all other considerations it may have some little weight in coming to the final decision upon the unfortunate men whose fate is now in the hands of the Chief Authority. Looking at their offence, and the nature, and the excitements to it, we trust we have offered enough to convince the generous reader of the justice of the principle by which all Governors of the olden time were guided in the matter of their gaolorship: that as the love of liberty was inherent to man, so also punishment for giving way to the impulse was equally ungenerous and unjust. That Sir John Franklin will so determine in the present case, we are perfectly convinced.

ACKNOWLEDGEMENTS

Nobody ever writes a book totally unaided. Authors are always in debt to publishers, editors, copyeditors, friends who read the manuscript and make suggestions, and not least to family who forgive you as you disappear straight after breakfast and emerge occasionally for coffee and a bit of grunted conversation before disappearing again until nightfall. Meanwhile, the vegetable bed goes unweeded, the refrigerator remains iced up and the kitchen tap keeps dripping.

Author's back-up teams regularly include researchers, librarians, website designers and fellow authors who have travelled the same path. There are map-makers, cover designers, publicity directors, printers, booksellers, wholesalers, literary agents, journalists, radio hosts, TV presenters and old mates who wonder if you remember them, but they got in touch because they've read your books and they had a great idea for your next one. (That's how I came to write *A Good Place to Hide*. Thanks again, Winton.)

So the list of people to acknowledge and thank for their help with *Ten Rogues* is long and disparate. My regular editor

Angela Handley deserves special mention, because she has the uncanny knack of knowing what my books *ought* to be like, and then bending and shaping them until they conform.

I've already thanked Professor Hamish Maxwell-Stewart in the Introduction for opening my eyes to the importance of the sheer gutsiness of the convicts. What I didn't say there, but will say now, is that he was endlessly patient with my niggling emailed queries. These descended to the trivial level of asking him if he could read a bit of handwriting that had eluded me in the early convict conduct records. (He could.)

I owe a special debt to Madeleine Blumer, my Chilean researcher. As I have already said, she was trying to establish the fate of people whose very lives depended on disappearing without trace. The fact that they largely succeeded is a tribute to their ingenuity and persistent cunning. Nevertheless, Madeleine managed to come up with credible Chilean traces of three of the ten rogues: Jimmy Porter, John Barker and James Leslie. In doing so she succeeded where others have singularly failed. Madeleine is the granddaughter of my old Australian friend Kate Metcalfe, and Madeleine and her family have lived in Chile for most of Madeleine's life. I was lucky to have her as an ally.

There are people to thank whose names I will never know. Electronic scanning of every page of the handwritten Tasmanian convict records must have taken an army of people a long time. Then the techies came along and catalogued these scans and made them available and searchable online. I live in France, and I was able to access these records easily whenever I liked despite the thousands of kilometres of ocean between me and the original. So if you were involved in this scanning operation, or in creating the website, then whoever you are and wherever you are, please accept my grateful thanks.

I should also put in a special word of thanks to Fiona Inglis of Curtis Brown Australia, my agent. I worked as a literary agent for more than a decade, and actually started Curtis Brown Australia where Fiona is now head *honcho*. Through three books I thought I didn't need an agent and could sort out contracts myself. And I could. But then I realised I was spending so much time messing about ineffectually on rights sales and mythical film deals that I wasn't actually *writing*. Fiona is an agent after my own heart, and she gladly took all these burdens away from me, leaving me free to write. Without her I might never have sat down and written this book. Thank you, Fiona. You're a star.

Finally, my heartfelt thanks to my publisher Richard Walsh, and to Allen & Unwin's managing editor Rebecca Kaiser. Apart from being the longest-standing friend I have in the world (we have known each other for 77 years!), Richard Walsh has an acute eye for a good story and has been happy to steer good stories my way, or to recognise them when the idea came from me. Bec combines those rarest of talents flair and good sense. Between us over the years we have managed to settle our differences and come up with last-minute book titles that actually clicked. *Merci beaucoup.* Thank you both.

BIBLIOGRAPHY AND SOURCES

Jimmy Porter left two accounts of his life. As mentioned in the Introduction, one was written in Hobart in 1837; the second was written on Norfolk Island in 1842. A slightly edited version of the 1837 story was published in the *Hobart Town Almanack and Van Diemen's Land Annual* of 1838. Some of Porter's story was fictionalised in that greatest of all Australian convict novels, *For the Term of His Natural Life*, written by Marcus Clarke and published in the 1870s. Porter is the inspiration for Clarke's character John Rex, and some of Rex's words in the novel are Porter's own, from his two accounts. And, of course, Porter is a central character in Australia's longest-running play, *The Ship that Never Was*.

I have largely stuck to the story as told by Porter himself in his two accounts, rather than copy some of the more colourful versions published elsewhere. If Porter was given to self-aggrandisement and exaggeration, then at least the exaggerations are his own. Insofar as these are the only accounts available anywhere of most of his life, we have no choice but to trust them. However, when other witnesses give independent accounts of some of these same events, Porter's version does match the witnesses' fairly closely. So he is not entirely unreliable.

The Norfolk Island version, from which most of Chapter 1 is drawn, is an odd document. The original is held in the Dixson Library in Sydney and is written in three distinct hands. It is impossible to know whose hand wrote what, though it seems likely that Porter himself wrote the last 60 of its 140 pages as the handwriting on these pages matches Porter's signature. It may well be that the remainder was a tidier transcription of Porter's original handwritten version, or Porter may have dictated his recollections for others to write down. Whatever the origin, I have largely followed Porter's version of his life story, much of which is in his own words.

The overwhelming bulk of this book comes from primary sources, some from Jimmy Porter's two journals and some from G.K.'s enchanting collection of memories, listed below as *The Sarah Island Conspiracies*. A great deal of primary information is available online. In particular, the handwritten Tasmanian convict records have been digitised and can be freely accessed at the Libraries Tasmania website: https://linctas.ent.sirsidynix. net.au/client/en_AU/names.

Exploring the convict records was not without its problems. For instance, just about every book listed below includes mention of a convict called William Shires and another called John Fare. I could find no trace of either in the official records; however, there was plenty of material on William *Shiers* and John *Fair*.

I decided to stick to the spelling in the original records, although I was assured that those records were compiled by barely literate people who wrote down what they heard, never mind what they were told. 'Shires' was more likely to be correct, I was assured. I was in the last days of writing the book when I found a reference to the fact that one of Shires's/Shiers's descendants had flown with Keith and Ross Smith on their 1919 pioneering flight from London to Australia. A bit more poking around on the internet led me to Wally *Shiers*, who had flown as one of two engineers on the Smith brothers' flight. Vindication!

As well as the convict records, early Tasmanian newspapers have also been digitised and can be accessed freely at trove.nla. gov.au/newspaper/?q. The convict records website is comparatively easy to navigate, but the Trove site, created by the National Library of Australia, is a bit of a nightmare until you get the hang of it. I wish any reader luck who wants to see the originals.

Jimmy Porter's Hobart journal is available for purchase online through the New South Wales State Library website at sl.nsw. gov.au/eresources. There is a fairly convoluted process whereby you follow a link into something called Ask A Librarian, and put in a request to see a document. They reply that yes, we've got it and yes, you can have it. Then you start filling in forms, giving them credit card numbers and so on. Eventually the document is sent to you as an email attachment. It's as complicated as it sounds, but worth the trouble!

The various books listed below as published by The Round Earth Company can be bought from bookshops, but also direct from the publisher. They have a website, www.roundearth. com.au/index.html, but no online facility to order the books. However, if you care to email them at enquiries@roundearth. com.au or call them on +61 (0)3 6471 7700, they will help you out.

BOOKS

Butler, Richard, *The Men that God Forgot* (novel), Hutchinson & Co. Ltd, London, 1975

Davey, Richard Innes, *Sarah Island: The people, ships and shipwrights*, The Round Earth Company, Strahan, 2002

—— (ed.), *The Sarah Island Conspiracies: Being an account of twelve voyages made by one G.K. to Macquarie Harbour on the western coast of Van Diemen's Land 1822–1838*, The Round Earth Company, Strahan, 2002

——, *The Ship that Never Was: The comic strip version*, The Round Earth Company, Strahan, 2002

Guarda, Father Gabriel, *La Sociedad en Chile austral antes de la colonización alemana* ('Southern Chilean Society before the German Colonisation'), Extensiôn UC, Santiago, Chile, 2006. (The two references mentioned in the text can be found on p. 674, note 162.)

Hughes, Robert, *The Fatal Shore*, Collins Harvill, London, 1987

Maxwell-Stewart, Dr Hamish, *Closing Hell's Gates: The death of a convict station*, Allen & Unwin, Sydney, 2008

Maxwell-Stewart, Dr Hamish and Pybus, Cassandra, *American Citizens, British Slaves: Yankee political prisoners in an Australian penal colony 1839–1850*, Melbourne University Press, Melbourne, 2002

Moresby, Admiral John, *Two Admirals: Admiral of the Fleet Sir Fairfax Moresby and his son, John Moresby*, John Murray, London, 1909

Porter, James, *The Travails of Jimmy Porter: A memoir* (Richard Davey, ed.), The Round Earth Company, Strahan, 2003

Rees, Siân, *The Ship Thieves: The true tale of James Porter, colonial pirate*, Aurum Press Ltd, London, 2006

PLAY

Davey, Richard Innes, *The Ship that Never Was, a Dramatic and Comic Re-enactment of the Capture of the Frederick from Macquarie Harbour by Convict Pirates in 1834,* daily performances at 5.30 p.m. at the Richard Davey Amphitheatre, The Esplanade, Strahan, Tasmania, www.roundearth. com.au/ship.html

INDEX

Page numbers in *italics* refer to illustrations

INDEX